Who Made the Moon?

A Father Explores How Faith and Science Agree

Sigmund Brouwer

THOMAS NELSON
Since 1798

NASHVILLE DALLAS MEXICO CITY RIO DE JANEIRO BEIJING

Published in Nashville, Tennessee, by Thomas Nelson. Thomas Nelson is a registered trademark of Thomas Nelson, Inc.

Thomas Nelson, Inc., titles may be purchased in bulk for educational, business, fund-raising, or sales promotional use. For information, please e-mail SpecialMarkets@ThomasNelson.com.

Scripture quotations marked NIV are taken from the HOLY BIBLE: NEW INTERNATIONAL VERSION®. © 1973, 1978, 1984 by International Bible Society. Used by permission of Zondervan Publishing House. All rights reserved.

Scripture quotations marked NKJV are taken from THE NEW KING JAMES VERSION. © 1982 by Thomas Nelson, Inc. Used by permission. All rights reserved.

Scripture quotations marked TLB are taken from *The Living Bible.* © 1971. Used by permission of Tyndale House Publishers, Inc., Wheaton, IL 60189. All rights reserved.

Library of Congress Cataloging-in-Publication Data

Brouwer, Sigmund, 1959–
 Who made the moon? : a father explores how faith and science agree / Sigmund Brouwer.
  p. cm.
Includes bibliographical references.
ISBN: 978-0-8499-2040-0 (hardcover)
1. Religion and science. I. Title.
BL240.3.B764 2008
261.5'5—dc22   2008027181

Printed in the United States of America

08 09 10 11 12 QW 6 5 4 3 2 1

For my friends Jeff Denham and Bob Barthel—thanks for your insight and your engaging conversations over the years, especially about science and faith.

And always, to Cindy and Olivia and Savannah.

Contents

PART FOUR—HARMONY

APPENDICES

PART ONE

Faith

Dear Olivia and Savannah,

Your questions about where the moon, the dinosaurs, and people came from are good, important questions. Your curiosity is one of the special things about you. I'm proud of you for wanting to know and understand God's world better. Only a really courageous person asks the big questions and dares to seek honest answers. I'm proud of you for being so brave, and I'm so glad that you told me about your questions.

These big questions are ones that people throughout history have been asking.

You will discover that some people decide that there is no God because it sometimes seems like science and the Bible can't both be right. If you keep looking, though, you'll see He actually uses both science and the Bible to teach us special things about Himself and about the amazing world. He's bigger than all our big questions, and if you and I search for the answers together, then we'll be able to see more of the special things God wants to show us. If you're ever worried or wondering, please come to me. In my own search for answers about science I've come to believe more and more strongly in God, and I'll be happy to help you explore your

questions. I won't try to make you believe everything exactly the way I believe, but I can help you try to make sense of whatever is confusing you. I love you. Always! No matter what you ask me about God or life!

The important thing is that when you wonder about God or you wonder about the Bible, you must not give up. God does love you very much. I want you to understand and believe this because nothing—absolutely nothing—is more important to me than someday being together with you and the rest of our family in heaven.

Love,
Your Daddy

ONE

Who Made the Moon?

Did blind chance know that there was light and what was its refraction, and
fit the eyes of all creatures after the most curious manner to make use of it?
These and other suchlike considerations, always have, and always will prevail
with mankind, to believe that there is a being who made all things, who has
all things in his power, and who is therefore to be feared.

—ISAAC NEWTON

Our family was gathered on the deck on a hot summer evening to listen to the coyotes. Nearly every evening at dusk, one pack would begin howling from the top of a hill to the west, to be answered by another pack from the east.

As the sky darkened, the top of a full moon began to edge over the horizon. It was a moment as wonderful and fragile as dust on butterfly wings. The rest of the moon slowly appeared, with the music of the coyotes as a haunting background symphony, until the silvery disk hung above the hills, so bright that the shadows of the lunar mountains were visible from a quarter million miles across a void, yet seemingly so close that Savannah, who was three, reached toward it and whispered, "Daddy, who made the moon?"

What an instinctive and profound question, embedded in our DNA. Even when we are mere toddlers, the night sky leads us to search for a Creator.

Indeed, *who* made the moon?

WHEN I LISTEN to the beat of my daughter's heart, a great, quiet love fills me. I do not say this because this sense of love is unique to me. What is incredible is that each of us is given a unique sense of it.

Of all the human loves, I believe this parent-child love can be the purest. I do not love my daughters because of what I can gain but because of what I can give.

How is it that something so invisible is so strong?

Why are we able to share love?

And most of all, where does this love come from?

THERE IS NO denying that the night skies speak to us.

Away from the city, away from all that is made by man, surrounding us and dulling our senses, when we stand beneath a clear, dark sky and behold the vastness of the stars, our souls respond like harp strings plucked by an invisible hand. We yearn with a homesickness to be somewhere else, an unknown place as difficult to define as the yearning itself.

Sometimes, in the dark, with my head leaning softly against my daughter's chest, a haunting sadness overcomes me. I hope that she will love me as much as I love her. I hope, too, that I will live until I am old. That I will watch her become a woman. That I will one day hold her son or daughter the way I once held her.

Listening to that heartbeat, I often think of how growing old takes me toward my death. Neither my love for my daughters nor their love for me will be able to turn away that certainty. So will come the day when, perhaps, one of my daughters will lay her head against my chest to listen to the frail thumping of a heart close to its final beat.

This is the human condition. Great sadness along with great joy. The more we love, the more death takes when it inevitably arrives.

How do we deal with this? Why is life so beautiful yet so cruel? Is there a purpose to this?

THE GENESIS ACCOUNT of Creation resonates so strongly with our souls because it simply and elegantly helps us understand the night sky and the longing that comes with it, giving us the answers to the questions embedded within us.

When Savannah is old enough to read Genesis, it will tell her that God made the moon. As she reads on, she will learn that her sister, her parents, and her future children are more than complicated packages of protein, carbohydrates, fat, and water, doomed to become dust when their life forces are extinguished. Because of the bedrock of Genesis, she, like me, will be able to embrace emotions that are uniquely human. Peace. Hope. Purpose. And from that foundation, the Bible will proceed to answer all of the other major questions of human existence that she will someday have.

> *The Genesis account of Creation resonates so strongly with our souls because it simply and elegantly helps us understand the night sky and the longing that comes with it.*

Who Made the Moon?

But also awaiting Savannah are answers that disagree with Genesis. Scientist and outspoken atheist Richard Dawkins would tell Savannah that God did not make the moon—or anything else. That the universe is random and meaningless. That we are merely assembled stardust. That our lives have no purpose—or hope.

In the introduction to his best-selling and highly publicized book *The God Delusion*, Dawkins states, "If this book works as I intend, religious readers who open it will be atheists when they put it down."[1] I was not. The book does make strong points against the flaws of religious institutions, and it demolishes poor and obviously cherry-picked arguments for the existence of God. But believers could, and perhaps should, do the same.

One of my goals as a parent is to ensure that by the time Savannah faces books like this, she will also be able to see that Dawkins does not have the intellectual honesty to fairly and squarely face the twenty-first century's most compelling argument for the existence of God:

Science.

An Atheist Undone

Antony Flew, perhaps the world's most famous atheistic philosopher, would once have also given Savannah an answer similar to that of Dawkins.

No longer.

Flew made global headlines when, at the age of eighty-one, he publicly renounced his atheism, having concluded that, despite what he had taught, argued, and published for all of his adult life, God does exist.[2] What would cause a man with so much vested in an atheistic worldview to make that stunning reversal?

Science.

Who made the moon?

That summer evening on the deck, as the last of the chorus of coyotes faded, it was easy enough to pick up Savannah and whisper back the answer. "God did."

It was an answer she accepted and trusted because it was Daddy's answer.

But almost certainly the day will come when she'll wonder if Daddy's answer is enough.

TWO

Through Heaven's Gate

I believe in God, the Father Almighty, the Creator of heaven and earth,
and in Jesus Christ, His only Son, our Lord,
Who was conceived of the Holy Spirit, born of the Virgin Mary,
suffered under Pontius Pilate, was crucified, died, and was buried. He descended
into hell.

The third day He rose again from the dead.
He ascended into heaven and sits at the right hand of God the Father Almighty,
whence He shall come to judge the living and the dead.

I believe in the Holy Spirit, the holy catholic church,
the communion of saints, the forgiveness of sins,
the resurrection of the body, and life everlasting.

Amen.

—THE APOSTLES' CREED[1]

One of the things I enjoy most about being a daddy is family
bedtime. After we read our two girls a story, the lights go off, and

my wife, Cindy, and I lie in their beds and tell stories. Each night one of us makes up a tale for the others. After this comes the family tradition of "favorite things." We each describe a favorite event from the day. And last come prayers.

One Monday night, shortly before Olivia's seventh birthday, instead of praying, she began to cry softly. She turned her back to me, and her body trembled. After some gentle questioning, I discovered why: the day before, at Sunday school, she'd been told that to get to heaven, she must love God and invite Jesus into her heart.

From our first prayers with the girls, Cindy and I have talked to them about how God loves us and that part of His love for us is the deep love within our family. We've taught them that Jesus also showed us this kind of love, especially on the cross. And they knew, by now, about heaven too because that's where Grandpa Cova went, and that's where someday we'll be together as a family, forever.

We'd never discussed that God's love and Olivia's own place in heaven were conditional, as presented by that Sunday school teacher. It had not been an issue—in her innocence and her trust in what we taught about God, Olivia had full acceptance and belief already.

But on this night, in the dark, our little girl wept, because she'd been thinking about the unspoken implication of her Sunday school lesson—the threat of what would happen if she didn't properly love God or invite Jesus into her heart. Since noon the day before, she'd been silently struggling with this fear. She didn't know how to "invite Jesus into her heart." Neither did she know, as she eventually confessed, if she could love God in the same way that she loved Mommy or Daddy, because she couldn't see Him.

For the first time, our little girl was afraid she might not go to heaven, and then she'd be lost to Mommy and Daddy and wouldn't be part of our family forever.

Daddy's Fear

Olivia and I shared the same fear but from opposite perspectives. In her future were school, the Internet, newspapers, and magazines—unless I was prepared to insulate her completely, outside of our household her faith would be challenged at every turn between that evening and adulthood.

I desperately wish to see my daughters in heaven. Our family love is so strong that I pray for it to remain unbroken for eternity. I cannot imagine a future horror of eternally grieving that they are in hell, however you perceive it, away from the presence of God.

> *Our little girl was afraid she might not go to heaven, and then she'd be lost to Mommy and Daddy and wouldn't be part of our family forever.*

Lost.

Since becoming a father, any headline that describes a lost or kidnapped child punches me with great emotional force. What if one of my daughters was lost, kidnapped? How could I get through a single minute, let alone through the dark of the first night, then the next and the next, until, God willing, our family was whole again?

How could I deal with losing one of my girls for eternity?

In nearly two decades of teaching writing classes to home-schooled students, occasionally I have met parents who are determined to cocoon their children from any negative influence. I often wonder what happens to these children at adulthood, when everything comes at them at once and they don't know how to deal with the world. Their defenses are weak because they've spent no time building their "immune systems."

The best analogy I can think of is the rising number of children with allergies. As Bill Nye, the Science Guy says, "With all our tightly sealed, filtered-air-system-fitted buildings; our hand cleaners; our detergent wipes; and our antibiotic soap, we have accidentally eliminated too many microbes or too many irritant organisms that, in years past, our bodies would have had to battle as our immune responses were programmed. Kids who don't get to play in the mud or the dirt, kids who aren't allowed to pet dogs or cats, kids who don't get outside much are, according to this line of reasoning, at risk for growing up with deficient defenses against disease."[2]

In the same way, parents who overprotect their children from conflicting messages and values leave them more vulnerable as adults.

In contrast, how much rejoicing once found!

Yes, one of the joys of faith is the sense of purpose it gives during our earthly lives. But another is holding tight to the promises of the Apostles' Creed, the forgiveness of sins, the resurrection of the body, and life everlasting, holding tight to the promise that Jesus gave His followers: "In My Father's house are many mansions . . . I go to prepare a place for you."[3]

But that night, at prayer time, our little girl had her doubts. She was genuinely afraid she might not go to that place. Yet Daddy was more afraid, because he knew he could not force her to choose faith when she became old enough to be responsible for her choice. He also knew that as his little girl grew older, she would encounter more doubts, much more difficult as obstacles to that faith.

What will be out there to encourage her to doubt a Christian worldview? Here's a list of recent titles that show a propagandistic attack on Christianity, all published by mainstream publishers:[4]

The God Delusion

American Fascists: The Christian Right and the War on America

The Baptizing of America: The Religious Right's Plans for the Rest of Us

The End of Faith: Religion, Terror and the Future of Reason

Atheist Universe: The Thinking Person's Answer to Christian Fundamentalism

In an article describing this trend, Rabbi Daniel Lapin points out that, with thirty similar titles, "there are more of these books for sale at your local large book store warning against the perils of fervent Christianity than those warning against the perils of fervent Islam." He added that "considerably more intellectual energy is being pumped into the propaganda campaign against Christianity than was ever delivered to the anti-smoking or anti-drunk-driving campaigns."[5]

But the printed page is not the only factor.

In a less tumultuous time, there were only three major news networks, along with the kings of print media such as the *New York Times*. All stood in splendid isolation, lighthouses, each seen by tens of millions. Then, competition became intense to reach the top and to have a voice, with a culling process largely based on talent, perseverance, and ambition. Continued credibility was one of the factors necessary to get and remain there. A voice of authority *had* authority. But the voices were still few.

Today, on the other hand, the voices are manifold. Our children live among podcasts, web logs, and Internet rumors. Where once stood a few lighthouses, high and mighty, now stand millions, of various sizes, all claiming to represent truth. No wonder it's more difficult to find a safe harbor in the glare of the lights.

Yes, it is more democratic to allow all of these voices a chance. But other than in major outlets, the culling does not take place. An opinion on the conflict in the Mideast, for example, can be offered by anyone, regardless of education and knowledge about the complex issues. Instead of the uninformed opinion stopping at the barbershop door, it reaches the world.

Andrew Keen, in his book *The Cult of the Amateur: How Today's Internet Is Killing Our Culture and Assaulting Our Economy*, writes, "Millions and millions of exuberant monkeys . . . are creating an endless digital forest of mediocrity."[6] He calls it a "pajama army"[7] and accuses it of spreading gossip and scandal.

Unlike the major media outlets, this army faces no checks and balances.

Do they have a right to be heard? Sure. Should you trust everything you hear from them and, by extension, allow your children to accept it?* Only if it also doesn't matter to you whether the

---

* Discerning readers are wise to ask the same about this book! Endnotes serve a valuable purpose, allowing my editors (and you) to expect a degree of responsibility and professionalism not common on the Internet. Once it is determined that the facts are correct, then the reader is responsible for judging the argument based on those facts.

surgeon holding the scalpel above your child has earned the right to be in the hospital. Authority must be earned.

My point is simple: the primary responsibility for helping children judge truth must begin at home, before they start their journeys through a digital forest of mediocrity. This is especially true when it comes to science and faith, where the shadows of extremists on both sides threaten to hide the light of truth in the center.

The Most Important Question

I believe there is nothing more important to ask than the question Olivia faced and wept over, even though she was not yet seven years old: what is your eternal destination?

Searching for answers often begins with an either/or foundation. We live in *either* (a) a godless universe *or* (b) a created universe, wherein God made the moon and our souls have meaning.

> *The primary responsibility for helping children judge truth must begin at home, before they start their journeys through a digital forest of mediocrity.*

Genesis is accurate. Or a lie.

Does God exist? Or not? Everything else is colored by the answer you choose. Even deciding *not* to answer is an answer. And how you understand this is the light for the rest of your experiences and questions.

Perhaps C. S. Lewis said it best: "I believe in Christianity as I believe that the sun has risen: not only because I see it, but because by it, I see everything else."[8]

But no matter how much spiritual peace and purpose a parent finds through a worldview based on the foundation that God exists and loves His creation, faith is the one gift a loving parent cannot force on a child. After a certain point, we cannot pilot our children's lives. But if we know where the safe harbor is, we must shine a beacon to draw our children toward it.

Finding the Right Light

When my little girl had been on a dark, stormy sea, worried about heaven, she'd trusted me enough to be her lighthouse. We are all drawn to beacons of light.

Not all lights, as you well know, are trustworthy. Seafaring history contains hundreds of stories of shipwrecks caused by scavengers using false beacons to lure navigators into treacherous rocks. The deception worked for two reasons. First, the very darkness around the beacons made it impossible to see if the light could be trusted. Second, the beacons were offered when the ships' captains were most desperate.

Our children, in their most terrible moments of doubt, are just as vulnerable to deceptive beacons. They, much less than adults, lack the skill and wisdom to discern false arguments. The result: "for the gullible and credulous, it is the confidence with which something is said that persuades rather than the evidence offered in its support."[9]

As a parent, you cannot guarantee that what your children learn from school, friends, the Web, and sometimes even church, is trustworthy. Furthermore, it would be futile and impossible to attempt to extinguish all the false beacons in this world. Our time and energy are much better spent in helping our children become like sailors who have the knowledge—experience, maps, and charts—to discern those false beacons.

With Creation, even if your own navigational chart to biblical truth begins with a literal view of Genesis, your child will someday need to know that there are different charts within the orthodoxy of Christianity. The purpose of this book is to help you understand those charts. It will not necessarily change your view on Genesis and science, but it will allow you to present, with intellectual honesty, what other believers have found in their searches.

If that makes you uncomfortable, I ask only that you finish this chapter before deciding whether the rest of the book might help you as a parent.

It's Not About You

Dr. Francis Collins is a scientist who journeyed from atheism to faith. A passionate evangelical Christian, he is the head of the famous Human Genome project. In his wonderful book *The Language of God*, Dr. Collins describes a men's dinner at a prominent Protestant church just outside of Washington, DC:

> It was an inspiring evening as prominent leaders, teachers, and blue-collar workers collectively let their hair down to talk earnestly about their faith, and to ask penetrating questions about how science and faith can contradict or reinforce each other. For a good hour of discourse, goodwill filled the room. And then one church member asked the senior pastor whether he believed that the first chapter of Genesis was a literal, step-by-step, day-by-day description of the origins of earth and of humankind. In an instant, brows furrowed and jaws tightened. Harmony retreated to the far corners of the room. The pastor's carefully worded response, worthy of the most deft politician,

managed utterly to avoid answering the question. Most of the men looked relieved that a confrontation had been avoided, but the spell was broken."[10]

In reading Dr. Collins's recounting of that evening, your own brow may furrow and your own jaw may tighten. After all, to get a feel for what it's like to hit a hornet's nest with a bat and watch the results, all you need to do at a gathering of believers is blurt out this question: was the world created in six literal days?

In the first draft of this book, I was like that senior pastor, hoping to deftly avoid the inevitable polarization. That is not the case with the finished draft.

First, that would be dishonest. You should have my disclosure right now: while not denying a six-day creation is within God's power, after years of searching, I see the harmony of science and the first two chapters of Genesis in a different light, without discarding the historical accuracy of the gospel.

In contrast, after little or much of your own deliberation and research, you may see Genesis as a literal account. Perhaps your brow is now completely crumpled, and the muscles in your jaw are popping. If so, I hope you find this second reason compelling enough to keep you from shutting the book: it's not about you. I've borrowed that from the simple and powerful first paragraph of *The Purpose Driven Life*, by pastor Rick Warren: "It's not about you."[11] Dr. Warren then goes on to say, "If you want to know why you were placed on this planet, you must begin with God. You were born *by* his purpose and *for* his purpose."[12]

You and I may disagree on how to view the book of Genesis, but *Who Made the Moon?* isn't about you or me. It's about our children, our common desire to help them come to understand

and agree with Dr. Warren, so that they too will have purpose-driven lives that lead to eternity with God.

> Could we consent to staking the faith of our children on where we **agree** on Genesis, instead of where we **disagree**?

Our children are growing up in a science-driven society, where it is far more challenging than it was for you and me to make faith decisions putting God at the center of the universe. Given that difficulty, could we consent to staking the faith of our children on where we *agree* on Genesis, instead of where we *disagree*?

The Grace Celebration

If you're still not with me on this, before you decide to permanently close the book, please spend a little time with me in an imaginary cathedral.

In this great and ancient stone cathedral, you are singing "Amazing Grace." You've probably already experienced the emotional shivers that come with singing the hymn with believers.

Amazing grace, how sweet the sound, that saved a wretch like me.

Imagine how much greater the impact in a building that has stood for centuries. Light shines through high stained-glass windows. One scene shows Saint Augustine.

I once was lost, but now am found. Was blind but now I see.

What makes this so special is that Augustine now stands beside you, his shoulder almost touching yours.

When we've been there ten thousand years, bright shining as the sun, we've no less days to sing God's praise, than when we've first begun.

It's a gathering of believers from all through the centuries. On your other side stands C. S. Lewis, and on the other side of him stands your son, and beside him, Dr. Billy Graham, with a comforting hand on your son's shoulder, both with eyes closed, lost in the moment and God's presence.

The music and the light and the high stone ceiling and the presence of God among believers swell your soul. Then, as the echoes of the magnificent hymn slowly fade, all of you begin, in unison, to recite the creed that was passed down by generations of martyrs, who paid for their faith with spilled blood: *I believe in God, the Father Almighty, the Creator of heaven and earth . . .*

In the power of God's presence, you see tears stream down your son's face. This, even more than communing with other believers, completes your joy during that cathedral moment. This is your prodigal son, who had turned away from the Bible—until he discovered a beautiful, harmonious way to reconcile Genesis with science. During those years when he was away from God, you, like the father in the parable told by Jesus, stood on your doorstep, scanning the horizon every day to see if each new traveler was your son, until finally came the day of his homecoming.

Now, in the cathedral, tears stream down your own face. The creed you share with your once-prodigal child reflects his full and vibrant faith in God, a return to the Creator who has transformed his life.

. . . and in Jesus Christ, His only Son, our Lord . . .

In the hushed silence that follows the shared creed, would it matter to you that, regarding the Creation account, Saint Augustine had concluded that "what kinds of days these were, it is extremely difficult, or perhaps impossible for us to conceive"?[13] Or that he had once admitted, "In interpreting words that have been written obscurely for the purpose of stimulating thought, I have not brashly taken my stand on one side against a rival interpretation which might possibly be better"?[14]

There, in that stately house of worship, would you also reject C. S. Lewis as a believer because you disagree with his assertion that the issue of a literal eating of the fruit in Genesis 3 is "of no consequence"?[15]

Would you ask Dr. Graham to worship elsewhere because he is open to considering that the word *day* is figurative in Genesis, while to you it is a literal twenty-four-hour period?[16]

After all the time you spent hoping that your prodigal son would someday find faith, would you tell him to leave the church and your household because he sees God behind the evolutionary process, while your knowledge of evolution ends at media headlines?

Or, respectful of Augustine and Lewis and Graham—and immensely grateful that your son is no longer prodigal—would you overlook your differences in understanding the mechanics of how God created us?

For it is by accepting these differences that you and the son you love can recite in unison, each with truth and honesty and sincere belief, the beginning of the Apostles' Creed: "I believe in God, the Father Almighty, the Creator of heaven and earth." More important, by accepting these differences, you can rejoice that you and your beloved child will share eternally in the joyful promise of your Creator as stated at the end of the creed: "the forgiveness of sins, the resurrection of the body, and life everlasting."

Amen?

THREE

Intellectual Honesty

It is not good to have zeal without knowledge.

—PROVERBS 19:2 NIV

A young man who wishes to remain a sound Atheist
cannot be too careful of his reading.

—C. S. LEWIS, *Surprised by Joy*

A friend who teaches at a Christian school once shared with me the poignant beginning to an essay written by a girl in the ninth grade. I paraphrase:

> *"It's time," Dad said one night in a serious voice. "Will you invite*
> *the Lord Jesus into your heart as your personal savior?" I didn't*
> *want to disappoint him. So I got on my hands and knees beside*
> *the couch and prayed with him.*
> *That's when I began living the lie . . .*

I have not yet read a certain Bible story to Olivia and Savannah. It's described in the tenth chapter of Mark, verses 17 through 22. I'm waiting for my girls to be ready to understand a difficult concept about God and freedom of choice. In this passage,

Jesus spoke with a rich young man who asked how to inherit eternal life. Because, since his youth, the young man had already kept the commandments Jesus listed, Jesus told the young man he lacked one thing: he must sell what he has, give to the poor, and then take up the cross and follow Jesus. As you know, the rich young man—although the Gospels tell us it is a sorrowful decision on his part—chose to turn his back on Jesus and walk away.

What strikes me about this story is the apparent callousness of Jesus.

The event in this story takes place shortly after the disciples had rebuked parents for distracting Jesus with their children. Jesus, man of love, was displeased and took the youngsters into His arms and laid His hands upon them and blessed them. He was anything but callous.

Yet the same man of love not only let the rich young man walk away, but used him as an object lesson before he was even out of earshot. Jesus immediately spoke with His disciples about the difficulties that rich people face in reaching heaven, clearly showing that He is more interested in helping the followers on the road to the cross with Him, than wasting energy on converting someone who has made a decision against the cross.

Cold.

The Son of God, as the Gospels tell us, was sent to earth to help lost sheep. Jesus, knowing He faced a tortured death on behalf of all the sheep, made no effort to save this one. Yet, of all people around the rich young ruler, Jesus was best qualified to make the case for choosing eternal life. Think of the tools that Jesus had at His beck and call. More persuasion, perhaps? A miracle performed right there on the road? Did Jesus do anything to stop the rich young man from turning his back on Jesus? Nope. Just a glance at the fine cloak undoubtedly gathered around the man's retreating back, then on to a conversation with the ones gathered around Him.

Stone cold.

Or is it?

Could Jesus have forced the man to "choose Christ"? Would He even have wanted to force that man—would He want to force any of us—to make that choice? No. From the very beginning, when Adam and Eve were left alone in the garden to choose between obeying God or sampling fruit from a forbidden tree, humans have been given free will.

> *If God Himself refuses to force His children to choose Him, then why should we futilely and wrongly attempt to force our children to choose Him?*

If God Himself refuses to force His children to choose Him, then why should we futilely and wrongly attempt to force *our* children to choose Him?

Choosing God

One of my goals is to equip my daughters to read the Word of God for themselves. I refuse to use the weight of my authority to make sure that my opinions on the Bible are accepted as the very Word of God. If I do that, then I am no different from a fascist dictator. Furthermore, without opening the door to discussion and questions about the Bible, it's unlikely that I will ever get a true glimpse of my children's inner lives and their doubts. Lastly, enforcing my viewpoints in a dictatorial manner would only be a temporary victory, because my power will inevitably diminish as they become adults.

No, if what I believe is true, one way or another, it will survive whatever doubts they bring to it. But if I don't let them challenge my views with their doubts, they'll never really accept what I believe.

In short, as a father, I want to help my daughters come to a point that when they read the Bible, it is not me speaking to them, but God. I hope to teach them to treat the search for truth as a lifelong jigsaw puzzle.

With a jigsaw puzzle, as you begin, all the pieces are scattered and confusing. The first thing you need to do is establish the corner pieces:

Random universe? Or created?

Who Made the Moon? is about helping your child see, through Genesis and science, that the first corner piece of truth is that God created this universe.

> *I want to help my daughters come to a point that when they read the Bible, it is not me speaking to them, but God.*

In the previous chapter, I described the evening Olivia told me that she didn't know if she could invite Jesus into her heart or love God properly. That night, in the dark, as I held her and marveled at her honesty, I prayed for wisdom. But I did not need prayer to know that I could not scold her for having doubts, or for admitting them. That would have sent the message that doubts are wrong. Savannah, a few years younger, who was listening with great interest, would have learned the same.

Harsh as it may sound, I cannot agree with anyone who condemns doubt. As Paul Tillich, one of the most influential Protestant theologians of the twentieth century, said, "Doubt isn't the opposite of faith; it is an element of faith."[1]

If doubt is wrong, then why was God so patient with Job?

Why, in Gethsemane, did Jesus ask His Father to remove the burden, questioning—perhaps doubting—the need for it?

No, as Olivia wept, I did not want to teach either of my girls to bury doubts. We all have them, even if we don't have the courage to admit it. Buried, doubts fester. Examined, they lead to truth like iron purified through fire.

Had I scolded our six-year-old for her doubts, I would have discouraged her from coming to me with any future misgivings. To whom, then, could she turn during her struggles to deal with other issues ahead in her life?

In the blanket of night, Cindy and I talked with Olivia about what it might mean to have Jesus in her heart. We told her that helping people who needed help and trying not to do bad things that hurt others were ways of having Jesus in her heart. As for how to love God, in the end, all I could tell her was that people struggle all their lives to know what that means and how to do it. That many, many people wonder about it all the time. That God understands this about us, and He loves us no less because of it.

I'm not sure these were the best answers. Nor, perhaps, were these the answers you would give your children at that age. But I believe that, as her tears dried and she stopped trembling, the *what* of the answers was not as important as the *how*. Olivia knew we loved her and would accept her no matter what she asked.

The Jigsaw Puzzle of Truth

In the jigsaw puzzle that is the search for truth, the closest we come to having a box top to guide us is the Bible. That's why it's so crucial to accept that the Bible's foundation—Genesis—is God's truth.

We are further hampered because not all of the pieces in front of us belong to the completed picture. We need to sort out what belongs and what doesn't.

Slowly, the picture emerges. Sometimes you know immediately where a piece fits. Sometimes you try to jam a piece in the wrong place. Sometimes you discover a piece that you thought belonged, doesn't. Often it is difficult and frustrating. Sometimes it leads to wonderful "aha" moments like when you pull out one piece and replace it with another and you see how well it fits. But assembling the jigsaw puzzle of truth comes down to how willing you are to prioritize, rearrange, or reconsider the pieces.

The Puzzle Reconsidered

For the first eighty years of his life, Antony Flew, British professor of philosophy, was a staunch atheist, legendary for decades as an icon and champion for unbelievers. As an author, debater, and public speaker, he literally built his lifework on the view that God does not exist. Not even C. S. Lewis in person could persuade Professor Flew of God's existence. During his college years at Oxford, Flew regularly attended the weekly meetings of Lewis's Socratic Club. Yet, on a philosophical level, Flew rejected Lewis's argument for morality—as later outlined in *Mere Christianity*—as a reason to believe in God.[2]

Then, in a 2004 story of global interest, at age eighty-one, Flew announced that he could no longer support atheism.

If you ever want to find an example of intellectual honesty, Flew is the poster child. He essentially renounced his life's works because of a new persuasion in his search for truth. (In evangelical circles, it would be the equivalent of Dr. Tim LaHaye's announcing that Revelation is not about a future tribulation and that dispensationalism is a flawed theology.)

If you have doubts about the existence of God, or if your current view of modern science makes you suspicious of it as an enemy of faith, you may find this interchange interesting during an interview between Professor Flew and Dr. Gary Habermas, distinguished professor and chair of the Department of Philosophy and Theology at Liberty University:

> HABERMAS. So of the major theistic arguments, such as the cosmological, teleological, moral, and ontological, the only really impressive ones that you take to be decisive are the scientific forms of teleology?
>
> FLEW. Absolutely.[3]

The scientific forms of teleology. Teleology is a philosophy or idea that holds all beings have a final cause or inherent purpose. You also may find of interest the reason Flew is open to going from deism, where God exists but does not take an active role in human history or life, to theism, where God does interact. From the same interview:[4]

> HABERMAS. Once you mentioned to me that your view might be called Deism. Do you think that would be a fair designation?
>
> FLEW. Yes, absolutely right. What Deists, such as the Mr. Jefferson who drafted the American Declaration of Independence, believed was that, while reason, mainly in the form of arguments to design, assures us that there is a God, there is no

room either for any supernatural revelation of that God or for any transactions between that God and individual human beings.

HABERMAS. Then, would you comment on your "openness" to the notion of theistic revelation?

FLEW. Yes. I am open to it, but not enthusiastic about potential revelation from God. On the positive side, for example, I am very much impressed with physicist Gerald Schroeder's comments on Genesis 1.[5] That this biblical account might be scientifically accurate raises the possibility that it is revelation.

Flew's father was a Methodist minister. I can only speculate on how his father must have reacted to Flew's rejection of God as a young man and then to his eventual reputation as "the world's most influential philosophical atheist."[6] As well, I can only speculate about his father's view on whether Genesis is an account of six twenty-four-hour days.

But if science and Genesis began Flew's return to God, then I can't imagine it would have mattered to his father whether they agreed if fruit in the garden was literal or not.

Filtered, Not Forced

If your view of Creation is close to a literal account of Genesis, in all likelihood you have already encountered the difficulty of reconciling it with what you know of modern science. But because you are an adult and have made a faith choice that will stand up to doubt, this is not a necessarily a problem. For you.

Yet it bears repeating: this is not about you; it is about your children. If you require that they, like you, reject the major teachings of science to have faith in God, too often they "will turn away from faith, concluding that they simply cannot believe in a God who would ask them to reject what science has so compellingly taught us about the natural world."[7] Sooner or later, regardless of what you tell your children they must believe, they will make their own faith choices. That is how God designed them.

> Because we can't force our children to believe something, our responsibility is to present the truth as well as possible. Instead of demanding agreement, we can help them search for the answers.

That is how He wants them to become part of His kingdom: through choices freely made.

Because we can't force our children to believe something, our responsibility is to present the truth as well as possible. Instead of demanding agreement, we can help them search for the answers.

Again, you may have a different view of the mechanics of Creation than I do. Because it's going to be very difficult to keep your children from hearing about the other perspectives of modern science, some of them from an atheistic worldview, wouldn't it be better if they discussed those perspectives with you, filtered through a perspective that shows how God is behind it?

If it's true that you can lead a horse to water but you can't make it drink, then it's equally true that if the water is pure and the horse is thirsty, it's impossible to stop it from desiring that water.

Our children thirst for truth. They will turn to you first for it. If you embrace and teach intellectual honesty, there is much less to fear about your child's faith decision than if you discourage their questions.

Keeping Antony Flew in mind, it doesn't hurt to remember C. S. Lewis: "A young man who wishes to remain a sound Atheist cannot be too careful of his reading."[8]

PART TWO

Science

Dear Olivia and Savannah,

You are precious miracles. No, really. You are! It's not just that you're such good, smart, funny people. I know you're miracles because the science that tells us about the universe also tells us that it's very, very, very unlikely that you or I or anyone else should ever have existed in the first place.

Recent discoveries in science have shown that the universe does, in fact, have a beginning. In the beginning, something came from nothing, and no natural law can explain how that beginning point happened. It has to have come from outside of nature. This beginning point supports the Bible's claim that God made the universe. This reassures us that He does exist, He does love us, and He does have a special plan for us

A famous mathematician estimated that the scientific stuff at the beginning of time had less than a one in 10^{123} chance of ever producing life. This is a 1 followed by 123 zeros. It would take you billions of years to count to that high a number. Another prominent scientist said that the chance of conditions essential to life happening by accident is about the same as billions of blind people solving a Rubik's Cube all at the same second.

Because of this, many people—including scientists and including me—believe something that rare can only be a miracle. This is one way that science shows us how powerful and smart God is. So, you see, you really are a miracle. The Bible already tells you this, but I think it's important you learn how science says the same thing.

Love,
Your Daddy

FOUR

Physics and the Miracle of Life

For the scientist who has lived by his faith in the power of reason, the story ends like a bad dream. He has scaled the mountains of ignorance; he is about to conquer the highest peak; as he pulls himself over the final rock, he is greeted by a band of theologians who have been sitting there for centuries.

—ROBERT JASTROW, ASTRONOMER

An explosion in a junkyard does not lead to sundry bits of metal being assembled into a useful working machine.

—FRED HOYLE,
ASTRONOMER WHO COINED THE TERM *BIG BANG*

I loved watching Olivia when she was learning to walk, to experiment with sounds, to chase our kittens. All of these things may sound mundane, but not to a father or mother. I was awestruck and grateful by this gift of life and of love.

Some nights, in the darkness when she slept, I would lean down and put my ear against her chest. I loved the smell of her skin and hair, the sound of her breathing. Most of all, I loved to listen to the beat of her little heart. Her existence was and still is a miracle to me. The miracle only increased when her sister, Savannah, arrived.

To describe my experience as a miracle is a cliché, a metaphor you'd expect, and hopefully forgive, from a daddy who is smitten with his little girls. The love that Olivia and Savannah have infused into my soul has transformed my inner structure and made me a new person. To me, that's a miracle.

Yet I also consider their existence to be a miracle in a literal sense, fitting a dictionary definition of the word: "An event that appears inexplicable by the laws of nature and is so held to be supernatural in origin or an act of God."[1]

> *The fact that we are here is a miracle in the truest sense. Inexplicable by natural or scientific laws, it leads us to realize that our existence is caused by divine agency.*

Why do I consider my daughters' existence to be a literal miracle? Because according to what has been learned through science about relativity and cosmology, my daughters should not exist.

I should not be here. Neither should you.

This planet should not exist either. Nor the sun. Nor any matter in the universe.

The fact that we are here is a miracle in the truest sense. Inexplicable by natural or scientific laws, it leads us to realize that our existence is caused by divine agency.

How do I know this with such certainty?

Modern physics tells me.

Quarks and Antiquarks

According to modern physics, in the first moments of time, when the universe came into existence, half of all matter consisted of *quarks*—particles that would later be assembled into atoms. The other half consisted of *antimatter*, called (naturally enough) *antiquarks*. When matter makes contact with antimatter, each mutually destroys the other, releasing tremendous amounts of energy.

Physics tells us that at the beginning of time, in the tiny but rapidly expanding universe, all newly created matter should have been destroyed by an equal amount of newly created antimatter. With all matter gone, nothing should have existed except endless, dark, empty space.

Instead, the inexplicable happened. For every ten billion antiquarks, the fledgling universe created ten billion and one quarks.

In trying to comprehend this, the closest I get in my mind is by substituting grains of sand for quarks. (It's a bad analogy, because quarks don't behave like sand, and a single grain of sand is planet-size in comparison to a quark. But most physics analogies are not quite accurate anyway.) I picture these billions of particles of sand by imagining the Indianapolis Motor Speedway filled to the top of the spectator seats. I then imagine formations of huge cargo planes dropping loads of "antisand," vaporizing every grain of sand inside the speedway—except for one, alone on the empty racetrack.

This single grain survived because the speedway held ten billion *and one* particles, and the airplanes only dropped ten billion grains of antisand.

Then I try to imagine this act of creation and destruction repeated almost endlessly until this tiny, tiny ratio of excess produces enough matter to form the planets, stars, and galaxies of the entire universe.

Much as I try to comprehend this, I can't get there. I can apprehend it, but I can't comprehend it. And I don't feel bad about my lack of comprehension; physicists have a difficult time with it too.

The magazine *Scientific American* posed the following questions in a 1993 issue: "How is it that so much matter managed to survive? . . . Why is there something rather than nothing?"[2] But while physics can raise these questions, it cannot answer them. Essentially, the reason we exist is beyond the explanation of natural and scientific laws. To me, that fits the definition of a miracle.

Miraculous Odds

The miracle of our existence goes beyond the inexplicable fact that for every ten billion antiquarks, the beginning universe created ten billion and one quarks. Why and how did this infinitesimal ratio of leftover matter assemble itself into the universe as we know it?

Roger Penrose, a renowned Oxford mathematician, estimated the likelihood that the four fundamental forces—gravity, electromagnetism, weak nuclear force, and strong nuclear force—would produce the conditions and energy distribution at the moment of creation in such a way that the universe would eventually support life. The chances, he calculated, were fewer than one in 10^{123}. This is a 1 followed by 123 zeros; to reach that number by counting aloud would take more time "than has passed since the beginning of time."[3] Another prominent scientist, Fred Hoyle, suggested that the chance of this happening by accident is about the same as billions of blind people solving a Rubik's Cube all at the same second.[4]

You don't have to be a mathematician to understand that these odds are beyond random chance. They are part of a deliberate design. To me, that fits the definition of a miracle.

Somehow, for every ten billion antiquarks, the universe created ten billion and one quarks. Somehow, against the odds of one out of 10^{123}, the universe grew in such a way as to make life possible on Earth. Incredible as this is, it is too easy to get lost in the abstractions of physics.

In trying to understand whether this universe was or was not a random event, it helps me to hear my daughters' heartbeats. This reminds me that I exist, as do they, because our bodies are composed of the dust of the stars. Carbon, hydrogen, oxygen, and trace elements are arranged in such a way that we breathe; that our eyes interpret light waves; and that our brains, in a mysterious manner, generate thoughts and give instructions to our bodies.

What an amazing, incredible process!

Is it so ridiculous to think that this world is moved by an invisible hand? That something—or Someone—created it?

Physics tells us that we are made of ancient stardust. But creation is more than that, more than the interplay of the four forces of physics that allows atoms and molecules to exist as they do. Each of my daughters, like me, was once a pinpoint of protein wired with DNA, growing into a complex organism according to the programmed direction of that DNA. I marvel to watch them grow, sustained by proteins, fats, carbohydrates, and water.

> *Physics tells us that we are made of ancient stardust. But creation is more than that, more than the interplay of the four forces of physics that allows atoms and molecules to exist as they do.*

More than that, all creatures are sustained because of the sunlight—not too strong, not too weak—from a star the perfect distance away from Earth. This sunlight allows plants that were once stardust to grow in the dirt. Not only do our bodies depend on these plants, but they also find nutrition in the protein of animals that eat these plants.

The life cycle on this planet exists because of sunlight and water and dirt, all possible because of the events set in motion at the beginning of time. It's that simple. And that wonderfully profound. Because we see it and live it every day, we rarely give this process any thought.

At times it may seem preposterous to think of an invisible, supernatural Creator. On the other hand, when I hold my daughters, I believe it is equally preposterous to imagine all this happening without one.

Science: Self-Contradictory?

We know from science that in the short time it will take you to finish reading this sentence, the medium-size star at the hub of our solar system will convert 2,400 million tons of hydrogen into 2,384 million tons of helium, spewing light and X-rays in all directions into the vacuum that surrounds it. In just over eight minutes, a tiny fraction of this newly created energy will reach our earth, where our atmosphere will absorb an even tinier fraction of it. The rest of the energy, which we perceive as light, will continue traveling outward from the sun at 186,000 miles per second on a journey toward the edge of an expanding universe.

Science indicates that our sun has burned and will continue to burn for billions of years at an incomprehensible rate of consumption. Yet the sun is one of *trillions* of stars, all spewing energy into the void. Really, our sun is normal to the point of being boring. Beyond our solar system are giant stars with enough gravity to rip our modest sun into a gaseous shroud millions of miles across, dead stars collapsing into black holes capable of swallowing all the light and material of entire solar systems, and supernovas violently illuminating entire regions of the galaxy.

With this in mind, consider that all these stellar glories lead to a disturbing contradiction that science has tried to address over the last four centuries: either there was a beginning, a point at which this vast amount of cosmic substance came into being from nothing, or it has forever existed in one form or another.

Both propositions are impossible in a natural system. Nothing in our material universe can exist without a fixed starting point in time. Neither could all this cosmic substance spring into existence from nothingness.

As you'll see in later pages, the standard explanation of the big bang theory rests on a "singular point" that is unexplainable with the laws of physics. In short, without contradicting the Genesis account, the singularity marks a time and place from which the universe sprang.

It should be noted that some physicists, such as Cambridge University's Neil Turok, while not questioning science's portrayal or accuracy of the events of the big bang, use string theory to challenge the singularity as a beginning point in time.

As Turok says about the big bang, "It's a creation event . . . if you talk to most physicists, they'd prefer that there was not a creation event, because there are no laws of physics that indicate how time could begin."[5]

To counter the singularity—not the unfolding of time that began after the big bang's singularity—Turok uses string theory to postulate *a universe that eternally expands and contracts, giving many big bangs in the past and many to come in the future.*

String theory, and a school of string theory known as M-theory, hypothesizes up to eleven dimensions and a universe built from one-dimensional vibrating "strings." It is highly controversial in the scientific community, as its opponents point out it cannot be verified by any experimentation, nor does it have any predictive power.

Furthermore, if used as an argument against the creation aspect of Genesis or the big bang, string theory merely sidesteps the question and answer of where, why, and how the first big bang originated.

Yet stars and the rest of the universe do exist. As do we.

I am among those who believe science should not ignore a third possibility: that the cosmos sprang into existence with the help of an outside agency—someone or something above the natural. The supernatural.

The Anthropic Principle

In the 1960s, physicists began to notice an extraordinary common denominator among coincidences in the laws of physics that could not be explained in any other rational way: the creation of life was only possible given the exact values and relationships in physics (more on this shortly).

Fast-forward to the fall of 1973, when a gathering of the world's best astronomers and physicists commemorated the five-hundredth birthday of the father of modern astronomy, Nicolaus Copernicus. Here a well-respected astrophysicist and cosmologist from Cambridge, Brandon Carter, presented a paper with a ponderous title: "Large Number Coincidences and the Anthropic Principle in Cosmology."[6] The contents of his paper were anything but ponderous.

Based on science that had been charted since Bertrand Russell's atheistic *Religion and Science*,[7] Carter argued what some astronomers and physicists had been beginning to wonder since the 1960s. He called it the *anthropic principle*, from the Greek word for man, *anthropos*.

If it is correct to say that there is a vast difference between inarguable data and arguable conclusions, then Carter's thinking is a good example of it. He gathered all the inarguable scientific data that related to the four fundamental forces in physics—gravity, the weak and strong nuclear forces, electromagnetism—that were necessary for the creation of life. Then he drew the conclusion that many in science were trying to avoid: Perhaps, said Carter, there was no coincidence to the number of strange and seemingly random coincidences that led to the existence of the universe and its life forms. Perhaps *all* of it had been arranged around one central task: producing humankind.

Physics 101

To appreciate what this meant, I needed a crash course in physics. I needed a picture in my head of the fundamental forces at work. Gravity? The weak nuclear force? The strong nuclear force? Electromagnetism?

I learned that all four of the fundamental forces in physics interact on an atomic level, which has profound consequences on a cosmic level. Quantum physics can give us a description of the atom, but it's much more complicated than what I'm about to present and must be truly understood through mathematical equations (which is why I prefer to rely on pictures!).

An atom contains at its core a nucleus of protons and neutrons bound together by the strongest force in the universe, the strong nuclear force. Electrons buzz in orbit around the nucleus, held to the core by the weak nuclear force. Although it's not quite accurate, think of it as a mini solar system. The nucleus is the sun, and the electrons are planets circling the sun. The main difference is that electrons don't circle in predictable linear orbits; they buzz at such an incomprehensible rate that it is impossible to predict or map their movement.

Atoms are so tiny that the smallest speck that can be seen under a microscope is wide enough to contain 10 billion atoms. If the nucleus of one hydrogen atom were the size of a tennis ball, the orbit of the single electron around it would be a sphere four miles across; while that might seem like a lot of space between the single electron and the nucleus, this electron moves so quickly that it has the effect of a fan blade moving with the power of a jet turbine.

> *This complicated interaction of all four forces is mind-boggling. But consider what happens if any of those fundamental forces is altered in the slightest. Everything in the universe literally falls apart.*

When the blades are motionless, you could easily put a finger in the space between the blades, but at full speed, the blades are essentially taking up all the space, and your finger would . . . well, you get the picture. The entire atom—consisting of its nucleus and an orbiting electron—is effectively, then, a cohesive and almost impenetrable sphere.

Hydrogen (with one proton and one electron) is the simplest

element in the universe. Uranium-238, on the other hand, has 146 neutrons and 92 protons at its core, with dozens and dozens of electrons at various levels of orbit, buzzing through each of their spheres of orbit at a fantastic speed that makes jet turbines look as though they're rotating at a snail's pace.

Every atom and every molecule in the entire universe contains this incredible, complicated dance of proton, neutron, electron, and all the other subatomic particles. The dance is played to an equally complicated symphony of music that is the perfect interaction of gravity, electromagnetism, and strong and weak nuclear forces. The consistency of this is predictable and unchangeable, as described by the four fundamental forces that science has charted.

This complicated interaction of all four forces is mind-boggling. But consider what happens if any of those fundamental forces is altered in the slightest. Everything in the universe literally falls apart.

Life—Hanging by a Thread

Roughly thirty years ago, after the big bang theory had been widely established, physicists ran computer programs that let them play God. By then, enough data had been assembled to allow them to understand the beginning moments of the universe. So they began to try to theoretically re-create the universe by tinkering with the four fundamental forces of physics.

They discovered easily and quickly that the slightest changes in any of the four would result in a universe devoid of life.

So far, this may not seem impressive in an argument for the anthropic principle. So think of it this way. You could win a state lottery this week. It's not likely, but if you did, it wouldn't seem

unbelievable. In terms of what is needed for a universe that produces life, call the likelihood of winning this week's lottery, as a
rough example, the same as the probability that gravity is exactly
the right proportion in comparative weakness to the force of
electromagnetism.

To be more precise, data shows that gravity is about 10^{36} times
weaker.[8] Without scientific notation, this number is: 1,000,000,
000,000,000,000,000,000,000,000,000. Gravity, the weak-
est known force in the universe, is this many times weaker than
the force of electromagnetism. Yet if gravity was only 10^{33} times
weaker, the mass of stars would be a billion times less massive and
would thus burn a million times faster. Life would not exist.

That's just one fundamental force that's absolutely necessary
for the creation of life.

Against All Odds

Could you win the same lottery again? Certainly it's possible.
Unlikely as it might be, "probability" means that you can't elimi-
nate "never." If the right constant of gravity is like winning the
lottery in week one, then winning week two is like discovering
that the weak nuclear force is just right in comparison to the force
of gravity, thus enabling a universe that sustains life.

The force that keeps an electron attached to the nucleus of an
atom is 10,000,000,000,000,000,000,000,000 times stronger than
the opposing pull of the force of gravity.

If the weak nuclear force were just slightly less than 10^{25} times
stronger than gravity, the attraction between the single electron
and the single proton in the hydrogen atom would be distorted
just enough so that all hydrogen in the universe would turn into
helium, with its two protons and two electrons.

No hydrogen, no water. No water, no life.

Now imagine the headlines after you'd won *three* state lotteries in three consecutive weeks. That's like the mathematical chance that, along with the relationship between gravity and electromagnetism and the relationship between gravity and the weak nuclear force, the strong nuclear force is exactly right to create this universe as it exists. But reduce the strong nuclear force by as little as 2 percent, and protons would not exist at the nuclear core, thus producing a universe without atoms. Reducing it by 5 percent means a universe without stars.

With that force exactly right to sustain this universe as it is, you've just won the lottery again.

But you haven't finished your monopoly on winning each week's state lottery. Number four in a row is like discovering that if the difference in mass between a proton and neutron was not exactly what it is, neither would be distinguishable from the other. Chemistry would not exist. Therefore, life would not exist.

Lucky, Lucky You

Here you are, the winner of the fifth consecutive state lottery, with the fact that carbon can and does exist. How important is carbon? It's the key element capable of fusing the long molecular chains of proteins, fat, and all other compounds needed for life, including DNA.

Yet, except for an astounding coincidence, carbon should not have the ability to form. Here's the physics: Carbon is number six in the periodic table of elements, with hydrogen, helium, lithium, beryllium, and boron coming before it. The math of the formation of carbon is simple. Take the nucleus of helium (two protons, two neutrons) and combine it with the four protons and four neutrons at the core of beryllium. The result is the six protons and six neutrons in the carbon nucleus.

What makes the formation of carbon possible is the ratio of the strong nuclear force to the constant of electromagnetism. Any variation in this ratio and it would be impossible for the binding of helium and beryllium to take place at the temperature typical of the center of a star. Why? Because, to make this possible, beryllium must be energized to an excited state where it is unstable enough to interact with another element.

The life span of this excited state is 10^{-17} seconds. In other words, a helium nucleus has 0.00000000000000001 seconds to find, collide, and be absorbed by a beryllium nucleus. And at this excited state, it has to match perfectly with the ratio of the strong nuclear force to electromagnetism, a coincidence scientists call astonishing.

Nitrogen, oxygen, and the other heavier elements required for life are built on the nuclear reactions that follow the formation of carbon. Without carbon as a bridge, the universe would consist almost exclusively of hydrogen and helium. Everything else, then, depends on matching the energies of hydrogen, the unstable

> *Astronomer Fred Hoyle admitted that his atheism was greatly shaken when he calculated the chances of this happening by accident. . . . "A common sense interpretation of the facts suggests that a superintellect has monkeyed with physics, as well as with chemistry and biology, and that there are no blind forces worth speaking about in nature. The numbers one calculates from the facts seem to me so overwhelming as to put this conclusion beyond question."*

beryllium, and the formation of carbon. And by the way, with all the forces that must be perfectly matched at precisely the right temperature for the production of carbon, this foundation of life is the fourth most abundant element in the universe.

Random coincidence?

Astronomer Fred Hoyle admitted that his atheism was greatly shaken when he calculated the chances of this happening by accident. In the November 1981 issue of *Engineering and Science,* he wrote, "A common sense interpretation of the facts suggests that a superintellect has monkeyed with physics, as well as with chemistry and biology, and that there are no blind forces worth speaking about in nature. The numbers one calculates from the facts seem to me so overwhelming as to put this conclusion beyond question."[9]

And the list of improbabilities continues. At a cosmic level, the ratio between the initial velocity of the big bang—the explosion that began the universe from a point of nothingness—and the force of gravity was perfect for the formation of the universe. Had gravity been stronger or the velocity less, the universe would have collapsed upon itself. Too much velocity or too little gravity, and all matter would have expanded too quickly for the stars and galaxies to form.

How fine was this difference? The world's most recognized cosmologist, Stephen Hawking, commented on the same issue:

"Why did the universe start out with so nearly the critical rate of expansion that separates models that recollapse from those that go on expanding forever, so that even now . . . it is still expanding at the critical rate? If the rate of expansion one second after the big bang had been smaller by even one part in a hundred thousand million, the universe would have recollapsed before it ever reached its present state."[10]

British physicist Paul Davies writes, "Such stunning accuracy is surely one of the great mysteries of cosmology."[11]

Indeed.

Want mystery and "coincidence" at the beginning of Creation? Astronomer Fred Hoyle wrote this:

> Even in its supposedly first second [of existence] the universe . . . *has to know in advance what it is going to be before it knows how to start itself.* For in accordance to the Big Bang Theory, for instance, at a time of 10^{-43} seconds, the universe has to know how many types of neutrino [a subatomic particle that has no electrical charge] there are going to be at the time of 1 second. This is so in order that it starts off expanding at the right rate to fit the eventual number of neutrino types.[12]

This is what it takes, then, to believe the universe was not created. Without even addressing why or how the universe suddenly sprang into being, you need to accept the fact that the universe had to somehow know ahead of time how it was going to evolve, and that it had to fine-tune all of these fundamental forces in relationship to the others. That's just to create a universe that would successfully remain in existence.

The set of circumstances is even more incredible for our planet to exist as a tiny and fragile life-containing bubble floating in the cosmic extremes of the rest of the universe.

The Whole Ball of Wax

Scientists estimate that the probability of the creation of the proper atmosphere with the coinciding establishment of the water cycle during the creation of Earth is one in a hundred trillion trillion (one in 10^{26}). How distinctive and unlikely does this factor alone make the existence of life on Earth? Among the hundred billion stars in our galaxy, and the hundred billion other galaxies (multiply those two numbers by each other!), a generous estimate of other life-sustaining planets has been pegged at a one in 10^{22} chance.[13]

A one in 10^{26} chance of getting the right combination of atmosphere and water means that if there were 10^{26} planets, only one would have that combination. But if there are only 10^{22} planets, the likelihood that this occurrence was random is reduced by a factor of ten thousand.

Forget all the other "coincidences" needed for life on Earth. We hit the lottery big time just to be able to have atmosphere and water.

But even more is needed for life to exist here.

Our planet's orbit is at exactly the right distance from the sun. From 2 to 5 percent closer, too hot. From 2 to 5 percent farther away, too cold. Most planets in our solar system have elliptical orbits that vary that much in either direction. If Earth had the same type of orbit, even at an average of the perfect ninety-three million miles from the sun, the seasonal variations in our planetary temperature would extinguish life as we know it.

Our planet's orbit is the exception. Nearly a perfect circle. And the tilt of our planet to the sun is exactly the right angle to foster life.

Picture-Perfect

Coddled at the perfect distance from our energy source, we live on a planet with a temperature variation that is negligible compared to temperatures in the rest of the universe, which vary from near absolute zero to millions of degrees.

Life here depends not only on a hospitable landscape produced by this extremely narrow and unlikely temperature range but also on chemical reactions that can happen only within the shield that Earth's atmosphere gives us. It's a bubble so cosmically minute that it is almost frightening to consider.

The universe extends for billions of light-years in every direction. (A light-year is the distance that light will travel at the speed of 186,000 miles per second in one year.) Yet it takes only sixty miles of upward travel to exit the bubble of life-giving atmosphere that protects us from the frigidness of that vacuum around us.

Consider also the following:

A slower or faster rotation of Earth eliminates life.

A smaller or larger Earth eliminates life.

A smaller or larger moon eliminates life.

A thinner or thicker crust eliminates life.

A lesser or greater ratio of oxygen to nitrogen eliminates life.

A lesser or greater amount of ozone eliminates life.

Not to mention the unique properties of water, the only known substance with a solid phase less dense than its liquid phase. If ice didn't float, there would be no marine life. But the microscopic properties of water are the truly amazing ones, allowing it to shape proteins and nucleic acids in DNA.

Water, the substance most needed for life as we know it, is also the most abundant molecule on our planet.

It's All About You—and Me

Could you win the lottery ten weeks in a row? Twenty weeks in a row? Every week for a year? Say the odds of winning once are one in 10^7, or one in ten million. Then the odds of winning twice in a row are one in 10^{14}, or one in a hundred thousand billion.

Mathematicians say that if the probability is less than one in 10^{50}, it is essentially impossible or beyond reason, for example, someone picking the correct lottery numbers seven times in a row. At that point, a mathematician would declare the lottery rigged. In essence, it would no longer be a game of chance but something that happened by design.

The essential argument of the anthropic principle is this: the mathematical probability of the staggering number of physics coincidences it takes for a life-sustaining universe to exist cannot be reasonably accounted for by randomness. In effect, from a scientific point of view, the supporters of the anthropic principle tell us that *humanity* is apparently the goal of the universe.

From a scientific point of view, the supporters of the anthropic principle tell us that **humanity** *is apparently the goal of the universe.*

Charles Colson gives us another way of thinking about it.

You could go for a hike in the mountains and by chance see a rock that, viewed from exactly the right angle, looks like a giant nose. Later, perhaps, you could imagine an ear from the shape of another overhanging boulder. A chin somewhere else. And so on.

We would agree that these are coincidences—random chances that wind and water had happened to shape in certain ways. But if you saw all the parts carved perfectly, no matter what angle you viewed them from, then saw all the parts assembled perfectly to form a giant human face on the side of a mountain—like those at Mount Rushmore—you would never believe chance had managed to shape it.[14] You would declare that it had been designed.

The Glynn Analogy

In his book *God: The Evidence*, Patrick Glynn compares modern science's discovery of the random universe to the "discovery" of America by Columbus.[15] Because Columbus had been looking for Asia, he assumed that America was Asia. Later, as the exploration continued, it finally became clear that the newly discovered land was not Asia at all but a new and glorious continent.

I like Glynn's analogy.

Over the past several centuries, science has assumed that our universe came into existence randomly and without purpose, and until recently, scientific evidence pointed to this conclusion. But now that scientists have begun to explore more and more of the universe, many are coming to a radically different conviction. Many scientists are realizing what Galileo, the father of modern science, always believed: the sun we see every morning was set in the sky by a Creator.

FIVE

In the Beginning

If the universe began with a hot Big Bang, then such an explosion would have left a relic. Find me a fossil of this Big Bang.[1]

—FRED HOYLE, ASTRONOMER

In the 1940s, Fred Hoyle was on safe ground. Until the big bang theory could no longer be reasonably disputed, the theory of the steady state universe—a universe that has existed forever—had been favored by science since Aristotle first proclaimed that something could not be created from nothing. As such, the steady state universe stood in direct opposition to any account that told us God was responsible for Creation.

But if Hoyle had intended to mock the concept of a universe with a beginning, he failed in a way that perhaps God intended with some humor. The name that Hoyle derisively coined for the theory during a radio broadcast is how it has been remembered since its validation. More ironic, Hoyle's challenge to find a fossil of the big bang actually led to some of the theory's strongest proofs.

Today the big bang theory vindicates the Genesis account as an uncanny and eerily wonderful description of the incomprehensible; for Genesis, like cosmology, tells us that the universe did indeed burst forth from nothing.

The Big Bang Theory: A Motley Cast and Crew

Perhaps the best way to understand science's explanation of the creation of the universe is to learn how the big bang theory unfolded, a story almost as fascinating as the science that makes it so difficult to dispute. It involves a group of Dutch musicians on a train, a boxer turned lawyer turned astronomer, a genius named Einstein, an obscure Jesuit priest who dared to publicly disagree with him, Hoyle's radio challenge, and two Bell Laboratory researchers who wondered if pigeon droppings interfered with the satellite reception of their gigantic horn antenna.

As you might remember from your high school physics class, light travels at a speed of 186,000 miles per second. (This speed applies in a vacuum. Mind-boggling as it seems, physicists are able to slow light in different media to the speed of a baby's crawl.) But as fast as light usually travels, like sound it still has a *finite* speed. In a sense, then, we live in a permanent time warp, seeing and hearing events only as they have happened in the past.

Think of observing a lightning strike a mile away on the horizon. Because the delay is so tiny, for all practical purposes, you see the strike as it happens. In truth, however, you see an event that occurred 1/186,000th of a second in the past.

Because the speed of light vastly outstrips the speed of sound, this concept is more apparent from the delay between seeing the lightning strike and hearing the thunder that rolls from it. When the thunder reaches your ears, that lightning strike a mile away is about five seconds in the past.

The distances that light and sound must travel to reach our senses, then, affect how far in the past we can see and hear an event. On Earth, with the relatively short distances involved, this delay is only fractions of milliseconds when it involves the transmission of light waves. In cosmic terms, however, the vast distances that light must travel through the universe to reach Earth make the delay much more significant.

If the sun in our solar system suddenly went dark, for example, we would not know it for about eight minutes—the time it takes light to travel ninety-three million miles. But those minutes are nothing compared to the countless centuries that the light of most stars has spent traveling earthward.

Twinkle, Twinkle, Little Star

On February 23, 1987, a night assistant at the Las Campanas Observatory in Chile stepped outside for a break and saw a bright star he'd never noticed before. There was a good reason for this. Until that night, the star had been a lot dimmer. It was suddenly brighter because it had exploded into a supernova. But not that night.

From the moment that star had burst with the power of millions of hydrogen bombs, the light from the explosion had been steadily traveling toward Earth as our ice ages came and went, as our civilizations rose and fell, as our technology progressed from Stone Age tools to bronze and iron weapons to steam engines to the spaceship that carried the first men to the moon.

Finally, after traveling at 186,000 miles per second for nearly 170,000 years, the messenger of this event—light—reached us here on Earth. When the distance and brightness of this "new" star was confirmed, it turned out to be the first supernova observed since the invention of the telescope.

What other grand cosmic events have occurred hundreds of thousands or even millions of years earlier in different corners of the universe? We may find out any second of any night. We just have to wait for the light to arrive, long after the event itself has become ancient history. So, the farther away from Earth we can observe with our telescopes, the farther we can look back into time.

The farther away from Earth we can observe with our telescopes, the farther we can look back into time.

Generation by generation, science has continued to develop telescope technology that now lets us look into layer after layer of time; the history of the universe has been unscrolled deeper and deeper into its past. Astronomers are now able to successively compare what galaxies were like as far back as 10 billion years in time. They can literally see how the universe has evolved, looking far enough back that it is almost impossible to deny the beginning of the universe and all that it implies about Creation.

The Doppler Effect

The light that reaches us shows the handwriting of God across the universe. The first scientist to begin to decipher it was Christian Doppler, who discovered the effect named for him in Vienna in 1842.

Nearly thirty years before, while heating various elements, a

German lens manufacturer named Joseph von Fraunhofer had noticed predictable variations in the patterns of lines in the spectrum of refracted light from those chemicals. Doppler used this to go a step further, showing that the speed of a star could be determined by measuring the apparent change in the frequency of its light waves. This, in the unfolding story of the big bang, is where the Dutch musicians make their appearance in the most famous experiment to confirm the Doppler effect.

This experiment took place in a train station in Holland, conducted (pun irresistible) by Christoph Buys Ballot, who put a group of musicians on a train and asked them to play a constant note. As the train rushed first toward him and then away from him without stopping at the platform, Buys Ballot was able to detect a distinct change in the pitch of that note. Listeners on the train, however, heard only the one steady note.

The explanation is fairly simple.

As the train got closer, it took progressively less time for the sound to reach Buys Ballot. The waves of sound became "squashed" on the approach, resulting in a higher pitch. The opposite happened as the train receded; the lengthening gap between the observer and the source meant that the sound waves were effectively "stretched," so that Buys Ballot heard a lower pitch. Meanwhile, those on the train remained a constant distance from the sound, so they heard the same pitch. This squashing and stretching is called the Doppler effect. (If you want to hear it for yourself and don't have a train station and orchestra handy, observe the game named after the distinctive sound that results from that same effect: Ping-Pong. The ball sounds like a higher-pitched "ping" when you hit it, and it has a lower-pitched "pong" when the person across the table hits it.)

While it is much more difficult from everyday experience to

understand this same principle with light, once again, the vast distances of the universe prove to be significant for observers on Earth.

Light, like sound, travels in waves. But unlike sound, the difference in the "squashing" or "stretching" of light waves does not result in a different audible pitch. Instead, parts of the light spectrum change. Visible light, as demonstrated by refraction through a prism, breaks down into the colors of a rainbow. Shorter waves are at the top, or blue end; longer waves, at the bottom, or red end.

Christian Doppler realized the wavelengths of the light from stars could tell him whether they were approaching or receding from Earth. By refracting the light of different stars at different points in their orbits, he observed redward shifts as they receded and blueward shifts as they approached. Since then, for example, the changing red and blue shifts of the two stars of Alpha Centauri have been studied long enough to show that they complete their orbits around each other every eighty years.

For astronomers of the nineteenth century, the Doppler effect was simply a useful tool to confirm what they expected from the orbits they had already observed: the universe contains movement of individual stars and other heavenly bodies. But for another seven decades, no one thought to wonder about the movement of the universe itself. And when Edwin Hubble did, what he learned staggered the scientific world.

A Boxer's Breakthrough

Hubble was good enough with his fists to contemplate becoming a boxer, and good enough with his brains to study law as a Rhodes scholar at Oxford. But instead of making a name in a canvas ring or courtroom, he found fame on a mountaintop in California.

Edwin Hubble's goal in the 1920s was to map the universe

galaxy by galaxy. He gained access to the Mount Wilson Observatory in California, which at that time held the most powerful optical telescope in the world. By using the Doppler effect to study the refraction of starlight, Hubble identified not only the elements in the stars but also the direction and speed of the galaxies. He and his team confirmed, at no surprise to them, that analysis of light spectra showed hydrogen and helium to be the most abundant elements in those galaxies.

But they also noticed something else that was extremely peculiar and difficult, at first, for scientists to comprehend or believe. And around that time, halfway across the world, a persistent Jesuit priest was trying to convince Albert Einstein to admit to the "biggest blunder" of his life.

An Einsteinian Error?

Early in the twentieth century, the scientific world had placed Albert Einstein on the level of a demigod. For good reason.

Isaac Newton's laws of physics predicted how most of the universe functioned, but constant observational tests showed slight and nagging imperfections, such as the unseemly wobble in the orbit of the planet Mercury. Until Einstein, science had to live with the imperfections of a Newtonian universe. But Einstein's genius allowed him to understand that on cosmic levels, gravity and light and time don't behave the way they do in our everyday lives.

While Newton described gravity as the relational attraction between two objects of different size—hence the famous apple falling to the ground—Einstein revised it completely, hypothesizing that gravitational effects are a consequence of the influence of cosmic objects on a grid of space and time. Gravity affects the space around it. Furthermore, and much more difficult to comprehend from daily life observations, gravity affects the speed of time—and can bend light.

The mathematical equations Einstein proposed showed all this to be true on a cosmic level. Essentially, the heavier the object, the more of a "dent" it makes in space-time.

Space-time? Dents?

Stretch a thin rubber blanket among four people. Think of that as a grid of space and time. Then place a heavy cannonball in the center. Think of that as a massive star. The weight of the ball will sink into the rubber, creating a dent, with the ball remaining at the bottom, just the way a massive star bends space and time around it.

Now take a marble. This is a planet. Spin the marble above the cannonball, around the walls of the dent in the rubber sheet. If the marble moves too slowly, it will sink into the dent. If it moves too quickly, it will fly out of the walls of the dent. At just the right speed (think of a race car moving through a banked corner), the marble will maintain orbit above the cannonball.

Time and space are relative to the position of the observer.

This, roughly speaking, was Einstein's concept of space-time, which he defined through those mathematical formulas that, to the amazement of scientists, were proved correct again and again by later observation.

Time and space are relative to the position of the observer.

Yet Einstein's new view of the universe didn't quite solve everything.

Newton had not been able to explain why, if gravity worked as he predicted, all matter in the universe didn't eventually get pulled together into one big lump. Einstein's mathematical model—unlike Newton's—showed that the universe could not remain motionless. But because Einstein was convinced that the universe was eternal and infinite, he theorized that there had to be some factor that allowed local variations without affecting the overall constant and unchanging status of the entire universe. He called it the "cosmological constant," a weakly repulsive force to cancel any inward pull of gravity that would force the universe to eventually collapse. To make his calculations work perfectly, Einstein added this arbitrary and extra factor to his equations.

Because of Einstein's stature, as well as the way his other predictions had proved so uncannily accurate, those in the scientific world did not dispute him.

Except for that persistent Jesuit priest, Georges Henri Lemaître.

Logic á la Lemaître

In the 1920s, Lemaître was the leading theoretical cosmologist at the Vatican Observatory in the high hills south of Rome. If he could find a scientific way to support a finite beginning, then he (and the Catholic Church, which supported his research) would finally be able to argue that the creationist ideas in the Bible were consistent with the new knowledge of the nature of the universe.

As Einstein's theories about space-time suggested the universe ought to be gently contracting or expanding, Lemaître studied them with great interest. He knew that Einstein had added the cosmological constant to fit the current scientific prejudice that the universe was eternal. This, of course, ruled out a moment of creation.

Lemaître, unafraid to search for or see God behind the universe, simply removed Einstein's arbitrary factor from the equations. Mathematically, this allowed for the expansionary force to counter or exceed the gravitational force everywhere in the universe, leading to the model of a universe that was always expanding.

Lemaître mused further. If the universe was expanding now, then it must have been smaller in the past. If this was true, then the farther back in time, the smaller it would have been. The logical conclusion to this was a point in history—a very, very long time ago—when the universe would have been at its very smallest, the point at which it had been created, or the "primeval atom," as Lemaître decided to call it.

This was the scientific model of the universe that Lemaître—and his church—had been seeking. The universe had sprung and grown from that beginning point, like a plant from a seed. Two exciting things about this model seemed to strongly support it: it followed all the mathematics of Einstein's model and, better yet, it solved the problems of expansion that Einstein's model predicted.

Einstein's Epiphany

There was one problem with Lemaître's theoretical model: Einstein didn't like it. Unimpressed, he even went so far as to ridicule the notion of a primeval atom and a moment of creation. Einstein called Lemaître's grasp of physics poor and declared that it was obvious that the universe must be eternal, infinite, and unchanging.

Whom would the scientific community believe? Einstein? Or a Jesuit priest with a perceived religious agenda and a bizarre hypothesis?

Unknown to Einstein and Lemaître, Edwin Hubble was patiently mapping the galaxies of the universe.

On Mount Wilson, Hubble's team had discovered that all the spectra of light they analyzed from distant galaxies were redshifted, meaning the light waves from those galaxies were longer, telling them that every galaxy in every direction was moving away from ours. More peculiar was the fact that the farther away the galaxy, the more redshifted it was. In other words, as distance increased, so did the speed. Not only was the universe expanding in all directions, but it was an accelerated expansion! It wasn't that the earth was at the center; it was like one raisin in a loaf of bread, rising as it baked.

> *Not only was the universe expanding in all directions, but it was an accelerated expansion! . . . It suggested that scientists could no longer believe in an unchanging and infinite universe.*

If this was true, it suggested that scientists could no longer believe in an unchanging and infinite universe. For Lemaître, it was news that perhaps he had prayed for—scientific evidence to support his model of an expanding universe. But how would he convince Einstein and, in so doing, the rest of the scientific community?

As a result of Hubble's work, Einstein wanted to spend time with him for further discussion. When Lemaître learned of this, he arranged to lecture at the California Institute of Technology at the same time.

Lemaître found a chance to speak to Hubble and Einstein together. Step by step, he argued the theory of the primeval atom and painstakingly worked through all the mathematics.

Then Lemaître watched Einstein and Hubble and held his breath. Einstein, after all, was inarguably the greatest scientist since Newton and had earlier called Lemaître's theory ridiculous. Einstein stood and made his pronouncement. Lemaître's model of the universe was, Einstein said, "the most beautiful and satisfying interpretation I have listened to."[2] Moreover, Einstein admitted the "cosmological constant" had been the "biggest blunder" of his life.[3]

Those of faith—inside or outside Lemaître's Catholic Church— now had a scientifically supported moment of creation.

"Find Me a Fossil"

Einstein was now convinced that the universe had a beginning. How significant was this to him as a proof of God's existence? He later wrote of his desire "to know how God created this world. I am not interested in this or that phenomenon, in the spectrum of this or that element," he said. "I want to know his thought. The rest are details."[4]

But Lemaître's triumph was not without opposition.

Lemaître's model of the universe took the data from Hubble's work and projected them backward, not unlike running a film in reverse. He was able to use the current expansion speed, and by knowing how far the galaxies were from Earth and one another at different points in time, it became possible to calculate when all the galaxies had been together, some 15 billion years earlier.[5]

This was not the picture of an eternal universe but of one exploding from what seemed like nothing. It was the "seemed like nothing" that was most preposterous to those in science who were committed atheists. They correctly argued that Einstein's mathematics also allowed for a contracting universe. Who could really say for certain that our telescopes brought us a picture of the entire universe? Beyond our vision of an expanding universe, they said, another part of the universe could just as easily be contracting. Our corner of the universe could just be a minor bubble in a giant cauldron of boiling water.

Among these scientists was Fred Hoyle, almost as well-known and respected in scientific circles as Einstein. Hoyle's work was revolutionary too. He'd demonstrated that stars had life cycles; they could come into being, and they could also disappear. The implication was that various parts of the universe could behave in the same way.

Against the notion of the universe springing into being from something smaller than an atom, on a "day which had no yesterday," Hoyle showed that scientifically it was very possible to conceive of an eternal universe with changing internal dynamics. So Hoyle issued his challenge mentioned at the beginning of this chapter: "If the universe began with a hot Big Bang, then such an explosion would have left a relic. Find me a fossil of this Big Bang."

In 1948, shortly after Hoyle's challenge, physicists Ralph Alpher and Hans Bethe theorized that if the big bang had occurred, it would have generated quadrillions of degrees of heat. They speculated that this heat would have left an afterglow that should be detectable even after billions of years.

Furthermore, they argued, since the universe had expanded in all directions, this heat should be evenly distributed everywhere. It would be difficult to detect, they said, because their calculations placed it at only a couple degrees above absolute zero.

Yet if this background radiation were found spread across the universe, this would be the "fossil" that Hoyle demanded.

Fossil Found!

In 1964, just down the road from Princeton University, Bob Wilson and Arno Penzias worked as researchers for Bell Laboratories. To prepare for satellite transmission of broadcasting signals, they needed to clean up the reception on a receiver. They had tried everything, including removing pigeons that were nesting on the giant antenna. Nothing worked. The low-level interference seemed to be everywhere.

Someone suggested they call the radiation experts at Princeton.

At Princeton, a team was in pursuit of proof of the big bang's background radiation as predicted by Alpher and Bethe. They were almost ready to scan for low-level radiation in outer space. They had calibrated their instruments to distinguish this radiation from other, more powerful radiations. They had added what they called a "cold source" to compare it against the temperature of the radiation they were seeking. The ideal test setup was almost ready, so they took a lunch break.

The telephone company researchers had accidentally stumbled across what the Princeton academics had been trying to find: Hoyle's fossil of the big bang.

During lunch, the phone rang. Answering it would cost the Princeton team the Nobel Prize.

Robert Dicke, leader of the Princeton team, listened to the information that came on the phone from Wilson and Penzias at Bell Laboratories. They'd checked the strange interference against a cold source. It was 3° Kelvin—only three degrees above absolute zero. That was the temperature in every direction they looked in outer space. Dicke ended the conversation, hung up the phone, and looked at the rest of his team. "Well, boys," he said, "we've been scooped."

Later awarded the Nobel Prize for their work, the telephone company researchers had accidentally stumbled across what the Princeton academics had been trying to find: Hoyle's fossil of the big bang.

Lemaître's model of a created universe—expanding outward from a singular point in time and space—was almost complete in scientific terms.

But what was about to be discovered about the universe would make science fiction look tame.

SIX

Creatio Ex Nihilo

In the beginning God created the heavens and the earth.

—GENESIS 1:1 NKJV

"In the beginning God created the heavens and the earth" . . . from a point with no dimensions?

If so, this truly is something from nothing—the "primeval atom" model of the universe proposed by Lemaître in 1927. Backing it up were observations that confirmed predictions made by Einstein's mathematics of an expanding universe, the redshifting of starlight from Hubble's work that showed our universe expanded in all directions, and the "fossil," a barely detectable background radiation of the remnant heat of a big bang that permeated the universe.

With all this scientific knowledge in the 1960s, there was still some doubt. Theoretically, the universe appeared to be like a rapidly expanding balloon. To explore the beginning of the universe, then, scientists simply took a model of its current expansion and ran it backward and backward and backward. Like sucking the air out of a balloon that had been filling for 15 billion years.

The analogy isn't perfect, and there is one crucial and almost incomprehensible difference. Filled or not, a balloon is the same object; only its shape changes.

On the other hand, running the model of an expanding universe backward—like running a movie backward—made it appear as if all material were collapsing into itself. At the current 15 to 18 billion years of age, all this material fills the area as big as the universe. Far earlier in time, the size of a galaxy. Earlier than that, the size of a star. Fractions of a second after coming into existence, the size of a grapefruit. And before that, an invisible pinpoint.

Then, running this model of the universe forward again, it seemed as if the stars and galaxies and cosmic debris suddenly exploded from nothing.

The equivalent with a balloon would be like seeing the rubber appear from nowhere and watching it mushroom outward, then playing a video of it backward and watching it shrink until the rubber disappears completely into thin air. With a balloon, our everyday and commonsense observations tell us that this is so obviously impossible that it is not worth consideration.

How could all the matter of the universe be packed into a point of nothingness?

How could all the matter of the universe be packed into a point of nothingness?

Our own planet has a circumference of twenty-five thousand miles. How could it, let alone all the matter of our solar system, our galaxy, and the countless other galaxies of the universe be reduced to a ball the size of a grapefruit, let alone a pinpoint? Not only that, but the most realistic models of the big bang show that in all likelihood the visible matter of this universe comprises only 10 percent of all matter that exists—another 90 percent is dark matter, observable only by the gravitational pull it exerts on the movement of galaxies.

All this from an infinitely dense pinpoint that exploded with enough heat to be traced 15 billion years later?

Was the event of the big bang real? Or were all the theories, and the evidence pointing toward those theories, wrong?

One aspect of Einstein's mathematics implied that matter would collapse into a single dense point under the right circumstances. But he refused to believe it could actually happen. It wasn't until the 1960s that physicists tackled the equations, encouraged by other developments in nuclear physics that let them understand more fully how matter behaved at a subatomic level, and with the help of new supercomputers, calculated that if a star were large enough, it would generate such intense gravity as it burned out that all the matter of the star, as well as its energy, would be drawn into a denser and denser clump of matter until it reached that single dense point predicted by Einstein. Something this dense would swallow all matter around it, with such gravitational power that not even light would be able to escape.

A black hole.

Black Holes

Going into the 1970s, physicists were finally prepared to accept that this point of dense matter, termed a *singularity*, was real. In theory. But they needed evidence that matter could behave this way. For if such a point existed, how could it be detected across thousands or millions of light-years of space? After all, it would give no light. It would swallow all matter and light.

And there was another dilemma. More theoretical work showed that although the collapse of matter was inevitable, as predicted by Einstein's equations, it was clear that at the point of singularity none of the basic laws of physics would apply.

This was the paradox: the theory said there was a point at which the theory did not work. Could, then, black holes really exist?

A black hole consists of two things only: a singularity and an event horizon. The singularity is the point without dimension where all the mass is contained. It is surrounded by total blackness; not even light escapes. The event horizon is the boundary beyond which light cannot return. The larger the mass that is buried in the singularity, the larger the dark area.

At the event horizon—as on the edge of a vortex of a giant whirlpool—all matter is driven around so fast by the spin of the black hole that it can be hurtled billions of miles into space. Something with the gravitational pull of a black hole also bends light that gets near the event horizon but not near enough to be pulled in. A black hole also exerts a gravitational force on nearby stars, affecting or controlling their orbits. A black hole close enough to another star strips matter away from the surface of the star and releases huge amounts of X-ray energy.

With all these believed characteristics of a black hole, scientists did not have to see a black hole itself to finally discover one. All they needed was to rely on an ancient adage: where there's smoke, there's fire. They merely had to find a place where a black hole exerted most or all of its effects on the space around it.

By the end of the millennium, they found all the smoke they needed to decide the fire was there: Cygnus X-1. Cosmologists agree it is the first black hole ever discovered.

Pea-Filled Yankee Stadiums

A point with no dimensions that contains a mass thousands of times larger than that of our sun? How does the impossible become possible?

Ironically, advances at the quantum level in nuclear physics made it possible to understand what happens on a cosmic level.

In comparative terms, the distance between the nucleus of an atom and the circling electrons is huge. (As noted in chapter 4, if the nucleus of one hydrogen atom were the size of a tennis ball, the orbit of the single electron around it would be a sphere four miles across.)

As stars burn out, they no longer create enough energy to generate the pressure that keeps them from collapsing against the force of gravity. A star the size of our sun—865,000 miles in diameter—will shrink to the diameter of a planet like Earth, only eight thousand miles in diameter. Called a *white dwarf,* such a star is so dense that one teaspoon of it would weigh several tons here on Earth. (Think of a city bus com-pressed into the size of a golf ball.)

Yet a neutron star makes a white dwarf look like a puffy snowball. The white dwarf has the mass of our sun reduced to a ball 8,000 miles across; a neutron star consists of the 865,000-mile diameter of our sun compressed into a ball only 10 miles across. Here gravity forces the atoms to be so crammed that the orbiting electrons are squeezed into the protons. The negative charge of the electron is canceled by the positive

> *Advances at the quantum level in nuclear physics made it possible to understand what happens on a cosmic level.*

charge of the proton, and they form neutrons, all tightly packed together.

To give an idea of what this is like, astronomer William A. Gutsch Jr. has compared the area of a normal atom to an empty Yankee Stadium; its protons and neutrons are like peas on second base, with the electrons buzzing like gnats above the bleachers. There's a lot of emptiness within the atom.

In a dwarf star, while the atoms are packed tightly side by side, as if a bunch of empty Yankee Stadiums were touching, there is enough space so that the electrons can still buzz freely within each empty stadium.

In a neutron star, the atoms are so jammed together that it's as if the buzzing gnats have been forced into the peas, and the once largely empty side-by-side stadiums are each crammed to the brim with those peas. All the available space is totally filled.

How dense, then, is a neutron star compared to a white dwarf? A teaspoon of a neutron star, weighed here on Earth, would be 500 million tons.

In certain situations, however, not even the incredibly dense core of a neutron star will survive against gravity. When a massive star explodes as a supernova, its core collapses because of intense gravitational forces. If the core—just the core, not the giant star itself—is between 1.4 and 3.0 times the size of our sun, gravity collapses that core into the roughly ten-mile-wide neutron star.

But a core that is bigger than three times our sun—more than 2.5 million miles wide—will not be able to maintain itself against the forces of gravity generated by all that mass. Instead of stopping when the 2.5 million miles of material collapses to a 10-mile-wide ball with the density of 500 million tons per teaspoon, the collapse continues, shrinking the core even more. Within a fraction of a second, the core collapses to nothing more than a point with no dimensions. Not even light can escape its gravity.

The Singularity Bursts

Why is the existence of black holes so important to the theory of the big bang? Stephen Hawking explained to the satisfaction of his peers—and to the satisfaction of the laws of physics—that the collapse of matter could also be reversed.

If it is possible for something millions of miles across to collapse into a point with no dimensions, as already observed in reality, then it is also possible for such an incomprehensible singularity to expand from a point with no dimensions, bursting into space and time. And from the next fractions of a second of existence, to develop according to the established laws of physics.

This expansion, which Hawking proved through mathematics to be possible, was the big bang.

Here I would like to repeat the paradox that I mentioned earlier.

At the point of singularity—Lemaître's primeval atom—the laws of physics that make this universe possible do not apply. They do not exist.

Furthermore, nothing in science can speak to the causation of the singularity. Nor can science explain why it exists, why it burst into space and time when it did. Nor how space and time could not exist before each came into being with the big bang.

All this—as anyone must admit, grudgingly or not—is outside the realm of the natural laws that govern this universe.

As is God.

SEVEN

The Foundations of the Earth

Where were you when I laid the foundations of the earth? Tell me, if you
know so much. Do you know how its dimensions were determined, and
who did the surveying? What supports its foundations, and who laid its
cornerstone as the morning stars sang together and all the angels
shouted for joy?

—JOB 38:4—7 TLB

From the beginning, I admitted that this book is the result of my
search to reconcile my faith with the findings of science. To this
point, I have represented these findings as well as I am able, discussing—admittedly in a rough and general way—the overview of
how the data of science led to the conclusion of the big bang theory. (There is much, of course, that I haven't covered, including
the tremendous work with particle accelerators that has contrib-
uted incredible advances in quantum mechanics and the
understanding of the behavior of the nucleus.)

No matter how strongly the big bang is supported by quantum physics and cosmology, you can approach this theory with a
certainty that God exists and measure what science tells you
against this certainty. Or you can believe God does not exist and

try to answer the questions raised by the origin of this universe in another way. Or, because of your interpretation of Genesis, after reviewing what science tells us, you may choose to reject either the data and/or the implications presented in favor of a younger earth.

As for my journey to understand the science behind Creation, I viewed it from the foundation that God exists and that He, by some means I can never fully comprehend in this life, began the process of Creation. Accepting an older earth, for me, does not dispute the Genesis account.

Secure in my faith, the scientific journey gave me a sense of privilege to be able to imagine the incredible way God began Creation. If science truly were giving a picture of the beginning of Creation, it seemed to me God was finally giving us some of the answers to the questions He had posed to Job. It took particle accelerators and radio telescopes and satellites and the work of genius after genius over the course of centuries, but finally we had a glimpse of what God had chosen to accomplish.

> *Secure in my faith, the scientific journey gave me a sense of privilege to be able to imagine the incredible way God began Creation.*

The scientific journey is simply, at least for me, like seeing a sunset in an entirely new way.

In the Beginning . . .

In the beginning, science acknowledges, there was nothing. No space. No time. (Sound familiar from Genesis?) Then came the awesome moment when space and time were brought into being. (Again, sound familiar?) Science can tell us nothing about that

moment, for that is the moment within the mind of God. That is the unknowable.

The knowable, within science, occurred 10^{-43} (0.0000000000 00000000000000000000000000000001) seconds later, when the entire universe was smaller than a single atom, when the temperature was 10^{33} degrees Fahrenheit, where all of existence was pure energy, not matter. The only force in the universe at this point of birth was gravity. At this temperature, the other future forces of the universe—electromagnetism and the strong and weak nuclear forces—remained coupled to gravity.

Until 10^{-35} seconds after time and space came into being. Now the universe cooled to 2×10^{28} degrees Fahrenheit. Although scientific notation is coldly efficient for mathematical use, it sometimes fails to give a sense of the amazing and awesome, which in this case is 20,000,000,000,000,000,000,000,000,000 degrees. *Cooled* to this temperature! At this point, the strong nuclear force emerged from within the shadows of gravity. Matter didn't exist in any form yet. Only energy existed.

At 0.00000000001 seconds, the universe cooled considerably and was only 20 quadrillion degrees Fahrenheit (20×10^{16} degrees). Nature was about to become more complicated. Where there were once only two forces—gravity and the strong nuclear force—now electromagnetism and the weak nuclear force uncoupled. The laws of physics, which could not apply in the beginning, were now set. (These are the same laws with all those amazing "coincidences" that will allow the creation of the universe to unfold as it did in such a way as to sustain human life.)

In the first moments of time, the universe still remained pure energy, a blinding sea of radiation measured in trillions upon trillions of degrees but cooling rapidly as space expanded. And finally, at 0.00001 second, it cooled enough for energy to begin to con-

vert to matter. The first subatomic particles formed, particles that would eventually give rise to electrons and protons and neutrons, which would then form atoms.

How much energy does it take to produce matter? The relationship of energy to matter is found in E=mc², where c^2 is the speed of light multiplied by itself and m is mass. Even a tiny amount of matter, then, contains a huge amount of energy. Conversely, of course, it takes a tremendous amount of pure energy to create a few particles of matter.

THREE MINUTES AFTER time began—when the universe was many trillions of times older than it was in the state of pure energy—its radiation cooled to a few billion degrees. With the values of gravity, electromagnetism, the weak nuclear force, and the strong nuclear force established as they are, protons and neutrons were able to bond and form the first nuclei of atoms. Hydrogen and helium, with one- and two-proton nuclei, respectively, came into existence. As did a small number of nuclei of the next most complex element, lithium, consisting of three protons and three neutrons.

But the universe was cooling so rapidly that within twelve minutes the energy that permitted this fusing process could no longer be sustained. These were the only three elements in the early universe. The other eighty-nine natural elements would have to wait until billions of years later, when stars and supernovas would generate the heat to forge them.

IT WOULD TAKE three hundred thousand years after the beginning of time for the universe to cool to about four thousand degrees. Until this point, only the nuclei of hydrogen, helium, and lithium existed; the electrons that dropped into orbit around the nuclei were immediately ripped away because of the fierce radiation. But at four thousand degrees the electrons were able to settle into orbit around the nuclei, and the elements are formed.

Something else happened as the electrons joined, held in place by the weak nuclear force. Radiation was no longer impeded by the presence of all the free electrons. (Deep within the sun, at temperatures in the millions of degrees, a gamma ray is literally passed from atom to atom and takes several hundred thousand years to escape to the exterior, where it becomes visible light. Then it takes only about eight minutes to cross the ninety-three million miles of space to reach Earth.)

As enough hydrogen was massed into the bodies of stars, the gravitational forces ignited nuclear fusion, and stars began to burn. Then the galaxies of these stars formed. And after a billion years, the large-scale structure of the universe was set.

At the age of three hundred thousand years, the universe was no longer a blinding, seething hotbed of radiation. The "fog" began to disappear as the radiation traveled outward. Today, this is as far back into time and space as we are able to see. Everything before that is opaque.

After three hundred thousand years, with the subatomic particles falling into place, gravity began to clump matter. It was a long process. Finally, as enough hydrogen was massed into the bodies of stars, the gravitational forces ignited nuclear fusion, and stars began to burn. Then the galaxies of these stars formed. And after a billion years, the large-scale structure of the universe was set.

Now came supernovas, stars old enough and big enough to burn themselves into a spectacular collapse at high enough temperatures to form new elements, spewing forth all these elements that would make planets, including our own solar system.

As this material clumped in our own solar system, the earth was formed in such a way that water and atmosphere would sustain life. Around it, everywhere in space, remained the background radiation, the "fossil" heat of the big bang.

All this came from what was once pure energy, the ignition of space and time brought forth into existence. Like Job, I can only tremble and wonder in awestruck amazement at how God laid the foundations of the earth.

PART THREE

Conflict

Dear Olivia and Savannah,

How we view where we came from affects how we view everything else about ourselves, such as whether we're loved or valued or intended for some special purpose in life. When people began to question whether God created us, they also started to doubt that He cared about us. They began to think that we're all just a cosmic accident, people with no real value or purpose in the grand scheme of things. This depressing outlook has dominated the way many people have been thinking about things for the past few hundred years.

For a long time, people have struggled with whether to believe the Bible is true about science and if God created us. More than four

hundred years ago the great scientist Galileo Galilei was put on trial for teaching that the earth goes around the sun; the leaders of the church had always taught that the sun went around the earth, and they were afraid to think about his new ideas. They were afraid that if people started to believe the church was wrong about this one thing, then the people would begin to question everything else. But Galileo believed that everything science discovered was just another way of getting to know God better, and his courage still inspires other people to seek answers through science too.

Wise people throughout the world have been studying the Bible for thousands of years, and although on many points most people agree, there are still some things that cause people to disagree. The Creation is one of those passages where people have very different opinions about when and how the world was created. What's important for you to realize is that all interpretations of the Bible agree on who created us, and more and more science now points to this answer too.

With that in mind, let's keep talking about how science and the Bible might seem to agree or disagree. I believe we'll learn together more about how amazing our Creator and His creation are.

Love,
Your Daddy

EIGHT

In Galileo's Footsteps

I believe the intention of Holy Writ was to persuade men of the truths
necessary for salvation, such as neither science nor any other means could
render credible, but only the voice of the Holy Spirit.

But I do not think it necessary to believe that the same God who gave us
our senses, our speech, our intellect, would have put aside the use of these, to
teach us instead such things as with their help we could find out for ourselves,
particularly in the case of these sciences of which there is not the smallest
mention in the Scriptures; and, above all, in astronomy, of which so little
notice is taken that the names of none of the planets are mentioned.

Surely if the intention of the sacred scribes had been to teach the people
astronomy, they would not have passed over the subject so completely.

—GALILEO GALILEI

I have a soft spot for Galileo. Not the scientist but the man, who
had two daughters, just as I do.

When Galileo was a young man, he fell in love with a woman
in Venice named Marina di Andrea Gamba and entered into (as
we so delicately phrase it these days) a relationship. Keep in mind
that this was in the late 1500s.

Let me put it this way. When a girl was born out of wedlock
in those days, the baptismal record was apt to read, "Daughter by
fornication of _____" (fill in the mother's name). The father was
never mentioned, as if the sin belonged solely to the mother. So

Galileo's first daughter, Virginia, entered the world under a description bestowed upon her by the church: "Daughter of Marina of Venice born by fornication."[1]

Some historians believe Galileo simply did not have enough money to marry Marina of Venice according to the traditions of their day. That might sound like a lame excuse, but I think there's compelling evidence to back up the claim.

Marital status aside, the more I learn about the man, the more I admire him. As head of his family, Galileo was faithful to his obligations to his sisters. He provided them with dowries that allowed them to get married, leaving him with debt that prevented his own marriage. He also supported his younger brother, a musician who couldn't get or keep a paying job and who later sent his wife and seven children to Galileo's household for support. Galileo was so financially strapped that he had to open his house as a private boarding school.

However, he remained committed to Marina of Venice and had three children with her. Daughter Livia followed Virginia. Then came their son, Vincenzio. Three children over six years. Galileo later claimed that these were the happiest years of his life except for the visits of Giulia, Marina's mother. (Read whatever you want into that additional fact.)

When Virginia was ten and Livia was nine, Galileo was offered a prestigious position in Florence. To take it, he had to leave his household behind. Yet Galileo took both daughters with him. It makes me think their presence was more important to him than the potential that gossip had to ruin his social standing. And it makes me believe that his little girls were significant enough to him to be worth the logistical complications of caring for them while pursuing his career.

In defense of my perhaps wishful thinking, I would offer

proof that Galileo was motivated by love and that his investment paid off as he entered old age. You can find Virginia's testimony to the love she had for her father among the surviving 120 letters she wrote to him. At age twenty-three, she began one letter, "I cannot rest any longer without news, both for the infinite love I bear you, and also for fear lest the sudden cold, which in general disagrees so much with you, should have caused a return of your usual pains. . . . I beg you to be so kind as to send me that book of yours which has just been published."[2]

Galileo—Hero of Faith?

Galileo is most commonly seen as a hero for science in his battle against religious leaders, but I'd like to make an argument that the church should view him as a hero of the faith.

Yet wasn't Galileo the man whose trial before the Inquisition irrevocably divided the church and science? And weren't his proofs of a sun-centered solar system proved true, while the church irrationally continued to teach that the sun and stars circled the earth?

Yes. But if you keep reading, you'll realize that these are both strong reasons to follow Galileo the scientist in search of the Creator of this universe.

During Galileo's lifetime, science needed to be freed from the church. In the centuries before, the medieval church had not tolerated any assaults on its authority and proclamations. Science was imprisoned by an institution of religion and made rapid progress only after Galileo's showdown with the Vatican—progress that has led to many of the benefits we enjoy today in medicine, technology, and expanded knowledge.

But if the church was wrong, how can we credit Galileo for

championing the cause of truth? Well, let's momentarily recall another famous example. Martin Luther did basically the same thing in his challenge against the religious establishment and is rightly hailed for it.

If he were alive today, Galileo is a man I would follow. Defending the truth against the Inquisition took courage. Understanding the truth despite centuries of opposition to it took intelligence.

> *Galileo's honest pursuit of science never led him to doubt his Creator.*

But to defend and understand truth, first you need to seek it. This is another reason I believe Galileo is just as much a faith hero as a science hero. He was unafraid to test the truth of his devout faith in a universe of divine origin. This fact is well recorded by historians but often ignored by modern teachers of science.

It would be wrong to offer the strength of Galileo's faith as scientific proof of a Creator. Instead, I think it's significant to note that Galileo's honest pursuit of science never led him to doubt his Creator.

Another reason to follow in Galileo's footsteps is the straightforward and effective way he dealt with opposition. As a young man, he was mocked for his audacity in questioning Aristotle's previously undisputed and apparently sound argument that one of the purported characteristics of air was weightlessness. Things fell down because they had weight. Because air did not fall down, reasoned Aristotle, it did not have weight.

Imagine Galileo in front of his mockers, blowing up a leather bladder like a balloon and weighing it. Imagine him popping a hole in the bladder, forcing the air out, and weighing it again. Imagine the silence when the two measured weights differed. Imagine the grin on Galileo's face as he defied a stodgy establishment. (Of course, tactics like these earned him enemies, and he later paid the price for them.)

While Galileo is best remembered for confronting the church of Rome, which in retrospect is seen as an irrational, dogmatic religious establishment, I'd like to point out that in fighting for the Copernican view of the solar system, he faced an equally stodgy and powerful scientific establishment.

The Bite of Dogmatism

Dogmatism is rarely a positive. To be dogmatic is to be all or any of these other adjectives: adamant, authoritarian, dictatorial, doctrinaire, opinionated, imperious, insistent, intolerant, obstinate, prejudiced, tyrannical, uncompromising, and unyielding.

In the Middle Ages, covering roughly the four centuries before Galileo, Aristotelian science had become firmly established dogma. Aristotle (384–322 BC) deserves his reputation as one of humankind's greatest original thinkers. He began a school of organized scientific inquiry encompassing all disciplines, essentially inventing science as an enterprise. He was so good at it, so wide-ranging and systematic, that after him it was far too easy to believe that all matters of scientific significance had been covered. Aristotle's first cause of everything was God, so his science was blessed by the church.

Bertrand Russell, in his book *History of Western Philosophy*, points out that Aristotle's rarely questioned authority in science was "a serious obstacle to progress. Ever since the beginning of the seventeenth century, almost every serious advance had to begin with an attack on some Aristotelian doctrine."[3]

In broad, simple terms, the downfall of Aristotelian science was that it did not leave room for empirical testing. Instead of encouraging experimentation, the emphasis was on observation and reasoning, with the foundational premise that all knowledge could come from human senses. This led to conclusions similar to the one Galileo burst with an air-filled leather bladder.

The most famous instance of Galileo disproving an Aristotelian conclusion is likely apocryphal, but it is said that he dropped an assortment of different-sized balls from the Leaning Tower of Pisa. Aristotle taught that heavier objects fall faster than lighter objects. By using balls of different weights and measuring the rate at which they rolled down inclined planes, Galileo supposedly proved this teaching false.

Here's another example. By sketching sunspots after watching them through his telescope over a period of two years, Galileo concluded that the sun rotated once every twenty-seven days. Until then, many scientists had believed that sunspots were objects passing in front of the sun. Part of their reasoning was incorrect theology: God had created the sun perfectly; therefore, it could not have blemishes. (Galileo paid a price for his efforts. It is commonly believed that the blindness of his old age resulted from ocular damage caused by looking at the sun.)

In rebuttal to Galileo's theory about the sun, some accused him of having blemishes on his telescope lens or even deliberately putting the blemishes there to fool others. Some said that if light from an object such as a star could not reach the naked eye, then the light didn't actually exist, making the telescope an untrustworthy tool.

Does either of these responses sound like people clinging to cherished dogmas?

If Galileo hadn't had so much fun poking holes in Aristotle's theories, perhaps he wouldn't have faced the Inquisition. It's not difficult to imagine his glee when proving his scientific opponents wrong.

Galileo was a difficult man to defeat in an argument. To those who claimed that nothing was true unless you could see it with your eyes alone—in other words, that the light coming through a telescope did not exist in reality—Galileo simply pointed the telescope at the writing on a building miles away to show that it read the same with or without the telescope.

Science today is not without its own dogmas.

But the dogmatic—in the church or in science—are rarely silenced by reason.

Eventually the dogma of Aristotelian science bowed to quantitative experimentation. Yet science today is not without its own dogmas.

IN THE QUOTE at the beginning of this chapter, Galileo outlined three points about the relationship between science and faith:

1. The Bible is not a science manual but a divinely inspired history meant to show the reason for God's relationship with the human race.
2. God gave us the brains and curiosity to learn what He didn't feel was necessary to teach in the Bible, including astronomy. After all, aside from Earth, not a single planet is mentioned in Scripture.
3. If the Bible had been meant for use as an astronomy textbook, it would not have ignored the subject so completely.

In short, as Galileo pointed out in a letter to the Grand Duchess Christina of Tuscany in 1615, the Bible is a book about how one goes to heaven, not about how heaven goes.[4] Given his faith in a Creator, it's ironic that Galileo is commonly seen as the scientist who began the great divide between science and religion.

A *Little* Knowledge, a Dangerous Thing

Remember the old saying "A little knowledge is a dangerous thing"? One of history's eminent philosophers, Francis Bacon, added a twist to the saying, pointing out that a little science estranges a man from God, but a lot of science brings him back.[5] For me, though early doubts planted by science never led me away from God, what little I knew from school did lead to guilty discomfort with my faith. The little knowledge that I had then about Galileo was dangerous—until I decided to face my questions and learn as much as I could about science. In high school and university, I would never have guessed that following in Galileo's footsteps could lead to a reconciliation of Genesis and modern science.

Copernicus, Tycho, and Kepler

Tension between church leaders and scientists had been brewing for centuries before Galileo arrived. Roger Bacon, the celebrated thirteenth-century scientist, studied the properties of light and rainbows and described the process for making gunpowder. A suspicious religious establishment accused him of black magic, and he could not convince Pope Clement IV to admit experimental sciences to university curriculum. In the centuries that followed, church leaders began to view other scientists with equal suspicion.

A few centuries later, the church was under increasing pressure because of the Protestant Reformation. By the time Nicolaus

Copernicus had the audacity to disagree with the religious establishment and propose that the sun was at the center of our solar system, the tension between religion and experimental science was primed for an all-out brawl. Galileo happened upon the scene at this volatile time, much like an unwelcome cop stepping into a domestic-violence dispute. He got it from both sides: science and the church. But there's an interesting side story to Galileo's life. It begins with Copernicus.

Because of the church's position on cosmology, Copernicus knew his proposed heliocentric universe was dangerous and heretical, so he waited until he was on his deathbed in 1543 to publish his work on the subject. Several decades later, an introverted German astronomer named Johannes Kepler (1571–1630) embraced Copernicus's radical concept. Kepler believed the sun was a metaphor for God and that it was right for the universe to revolve around it in homage. Nevertheless, he couldn't make the theory fit the available data.

Smart man: he looked for better data.

Meanwhile, a scientist who had great data was looking for a better mathematician. The data guy was Danish astronomer Tycho Brahe, born in 1546. You may vaguely remember the Copernicus-Kepler-Brahe-Galileo chain of events from sometime in your school days. But I doubt your teacher told you about the golden nose and the burst bladder in this story.

Tycho was expert at collecting data. He claimed to be the greatest naked-eye observer of the skies who ever lived, and he proved his claim with immaculate records of the positions of planets and stars. When he was finally able to admit that he wasn't the mathematician he had once fancied himself, Tycho invited Kepler to work with him.

Their partnership was rife with dysfunction. Kepler was an

introvert; Tycho, a party animal. They didn't like each other, and Tycho fed Kepler only a little data at a time, just enough to keep him interested. It took Tycho's death for Kepler to inherit all of Tycho's data about the night sky. From this information, Kepler revolutionized the Western understanding of the universe by scientifically proving that planets moved in elliptical orbits around the sun.

Galileo soon entered the saga, and his agreement with Kepler resulted in conflict with the church.

Tycho, flamboyant reveler that he was, wore a golden nose. In his student days, he lost the bridge of his real nose during a rapier duel with a fellow student because of a drunken argument over who was better at math.

This disfigurement, however, didn't dampen Tycho's rowdiness. One evening Tycho attended a party in the presence of the Baron of Rosenberg. As usual, Tycho overindulged. Because he could not respectfully excuse himself from the baron's presence, he resisted his body's urges until his bladder finally burst.* He died soon after from internal infection, repeating deliriously to Kepler from his deathbed, "Let me not seem to have lived in vain. Let me not seem to have lived in vain."[6]

---

*In writing this book, I've learned that some doctors assert that a human bladder is incapable of bursting in this manner. Also, some historians suggest that Tycho died of mercury poisoning, not urinary tract infection. I point this out because I feel I need to be fair in the pursuit of truth. However, these counterarguments still leave room for the possibility that bladders can burst, and many historians recount Tycho's end as described. Because I'm a novelist and cannot help but love the dramatic aspects of the traditionally told version, I've presented the story as is, and I'm sticking with it.

Galileo's Warning to the Church

Although Galileo didn't invent the telescope (a common misperception), he improved its design and turned it heavenward. What he saw was the first clear evidence that Aristotle and Ptolemy had been wrong to claim that the earth was at the center of the universe. Copernicus had been right about the movement of the planets.

Galileo also anticipated the telescope would be adopted by other scientists across Europe, and the religious leaders in Rome would be proved wrong if they continued to proclaim that Copernicus's theory was heresy. To help prepare his friends in the church, Galileo wrote a letter to show that Copernicus's theory was indeed consistent with Catholic doctrine. The church, he stated, should revise its stand.

His prescient warning was:

> Take note, theologians, that in your desire to make matters of faith out of propositions relating to the fixity of sun and earth you run the risk of eventually having to condemn as heretics those who would declare the earth to stand still and the sun to change position—eventually, I say, at such a time as it might be physically or logically proved that the earth moves and the sun stands still.[7]

Mistake. Not his warning, but his perception of how it would be received.

Galileo had just as many enemies as friends in the church, for he had a quick and often sarcastic wit and a quicker impatience with those who could not follow or agree with his science. More unfortunate was the political climate at the time, characterized by the power held by the church's Inquisition, a committee dedicated to seeking and punishing heretics.

In 1616, Galileo was summoned to Rome to defend his letter. He was cleared of the charges of heresy and allowed to treat the Copernican theory as hypothetical but not true. Nonetheless, Galileo was ordered not to "hold or defend" the Copernican theory again. (I think this marked ambivalence shows that even in the church some saw no reason for a divide between religion and science.)

Sixteen years later, Galileo tried to walk that tightrope of discussing the "hypothetical" theory without declaring it to be true. In a book now hailed as a scientific masterpiece, *Dialogue Concerning the Two Chief World Systems*, Galileo compared Ptolemaic-Aristotelian theory with Copernican theory, merely emphasizing the logical superiority of the second system. Despite Galileo's carefully chosen semantics, the church summoned him to Rome on charges of heresy.

> *Galileo's verified scientific data had no dispute with the Bible or the existence of God. The dispute arose because of the nonbiblical claims of church leaders.*

In the church's defense, the validity of Galileo's science was not on trial. According to official transcripts of the trial, it was never even debated, but to his shrewd and gleeful enemies, the truth of Galileo's arguments was irrelevant. He had undeniably disobeyed the previous order not to "hold or defend" the Copernican theory.

The result is what I learned in childhood without understanding the politics behind it. Galileo was found guilty as charged. Because of the possibility, however unlikely, of being executed, he chose to publicly withdraw his statement. He received a sentence of life imprisonment, which he served in the relative comfort of house arrest in a Florence villa.

But the damage was done. His book was out there, and the controversy only made it more popular. Science had proved that the church's stand was wrong. The church lost its monopoly on "truth," and since then, religion has been perceived as an anti-science establishment where blind faith trumps clear evidence.

Here is, I believe, the most important and least-remembered point about Galileo's trial: Galileo's verified scientific data had no dispute with the Bible or the existence of God. The dispute arose because of the nonbiblical claims of church leaders.

In Galileo's Footsteps

It comforts me to know that I share the same faith with one of our most revered scientists. I love to imagine Galileo's excitement as he turned a telescope to the heavens, becoming one of the first to see the lunar mountains and impact craters as well as the moons circling Jupiter. He must have experienced the same sense of awe that my daughters and I feel when we look at the night sky and search for the larger planets and familiar stars.

It is fascinating to follow the trail of science that continues beyond Galileo's footsteps—a trail based on the scientific method that he helped establish—and discover how four centuries of cumulative searching have been leading science back to a universe with a Creator.

I admire Galileo's willingness to stand firm against establishment thinking. I believe he would also be willing to take a stand against the new establishment that has come into power. If once the church ruled Western thought, it is safe to say that today science does.

I want to believe that Galileo would challenge scientists who have a subjective predetermination that God does not exist. (At that point it is no longer objective, for it begins with a premise and, in direct contradiction to the scientific method, does not test it.) I think Galileo would invite them to apply the same scientific methods he established and search without bias for an answer to the question of whether we live in a random universe or a created universe.

If God did not create the universe, then science will show nothing to suggest a supernatural Creator. But if God created this universe, then He is behind all science. While scientific proof of His existence may be beyond our capabilities, at the very least science should *point* to His existence. And I believe Galileo would argue that it is entirely fair to openly consider what science has to tell us about the existence of a supernatural Creator—and *then* to accept or reject His existence based on the evidence.

> If God created this universe, then He is behind all science.

If you follow in Galileo's footsteps, you may be surprised to find how scientific discoveries about the big bang call into question a random universe—and how, instead, they strengthen faith. We in the church need to learn from Galileo's persecution, acknowledge the damage done by well-intentioned but misguided theologians who have opposed the big bang theory, and gain the sound scientific knowledge needed to respond intelligently to skeptics who use science to question the biblical claims of a supernatural Creator.

NINE

The Fence Around the Cross

Men are forced into strange fancies by attempting to measure the whole universe by means of their tiny scale.

—GALILEO GALILEI

I play hockey and golf with my friend Jeff Denham. Our families get together occasionally. I've warned Jeff that his name would be in this book, because I wanted to share a conversation that he and I once had about the age of the earth.

Jeff is a six-foot-two-inch package of contradictions. He's a charming rogue. His nose once collided with a puck and still has a bend where it broke the first of five times. He has the mischievousness of an eight-year-old boy and is better read and more articulate than most PhDs. He's a successful businessman in the difficult and sometimes cutthroat car dealership business, but he operates with obvious integrity. Jeff is a compassionate employer of dozens of people and feels responsibility for all the families supported by those salaries.

I suspect he was playing devil's advocate in the conversation I want to share. That's part of his mischievous character. Because of the competitive nature that once had him on the road to pro hockey, he was enjoying our argument. On the ice, his arsenal contains superior skating skills and a mean slap shot; here, his weapon of choice was his considerable knowledge base.

I was sitting in Jeff's office, where we were discussing when the earth had been created. We share the view that the God of Genesis had created this universe. But on that day Jeff had been arguing for a young earth only thousands of years old, created in six twenty-four-hour days, while I suggested an older earth, billions of years old, created in six ages.

As you may know, there is a spirited, passionate, and sometimes—okay, often—heated debate in Christian circles on this subject. This was not one of those situations. I wanted to learn how my friend could make a scientific case for a young earth, and it seemed as though he wanted to learn from me too. Given that the debate has been going on for decades without clear resolution, it should come as no surprise that neither of us changed positions.

Finally, I said that he and I would probably only agree to disagree, thinking this would be the end of our discussion. He nodded, saying it didn't really matter how old the earth was; what was important was what we had agreed upon at the beginning of our conversation: that God created this world. I agreed. And besides, Jeff went on, regardless of the Creation date, wasn't it incredible that God loved us enough to send His Son?

I was about to agree with that too, but was struck by something Jeff had said earlier, before our discussion of the earth's age. He'd mentioned that for his employees who weren't Christians, his door was always open to any questions they might ask about God.

"Jeff," I said with quiet certainty, "I think you're wrong."

That may have surprised him. Not once during our debate had either of us used "right" or "wrong." This had ensured that neither of us felt attacked.

"Wrong?" He frowned. When Jeff frowns, it is intimidating. If you want an idea of just how intimidating, tune in to a wrestling match and wait for a close-up.

"You're wrong," I continued, "to say that the age of the earth doesn't matter, as long as we know it was created. Maybe between you and me it doesn't matter, because we're secure in our faith. But I think it will matter when one of your employees steps into this office and wants to know more about God."

"What do you mean?" Jeff asked.

"Some people can accept on faith, contrary to the evidence presented by modern science, that this is a young earth. When I said that the Grand Canyon proves that the earth is older than seven thousand years, you countered by saying the earth could have been created looking as old as it does. But it takes faith to reject the self-evident answer and choose the one more difficult to believe, right?"

"If the Bible says it's true . . ."

"You know the Bible is true, and I know the Bible is true," I said. "But someone stepping into your office, searching for God, isn't operating with that premise. Otherwise that person wouldn't be searching."

"Fair enough."

"So one of your employees is down on life and feels there is no hope, and you want to tell this person that the Cross is the answer, but before he gets there, he has to believe the earth is only seven thousand years old, because that's what Genesis says. Do you think that's going to make it easy for the discussion to continue a faith search?"

I paused. "Here's where I'd say the age of the earth does matter."

Jeff blinked a few times and for the first time had no quick counterpoint. After a few more seconds, it became apparent that he wasn't going to disagree.

"Insisting on an earth only a few thousand years old is a big fence around the Cross," I finished, still quiet. "It makes me wonder how many people in our culture have been kept away because of it."

He nodded, still silent. I hadn't won the debate or changed his mind about the age of the earth, but we had both come to realize something very, very important.

Faith for Our Children

The great scientist Galileo Galilei spent his life searching for scientific truth. He risked his life to defend it. And it never caused him to doubt his faith in a God who created this universe. Many of the political troubles that filled the end of his life began because he boldly stated, "Since no two truths can contradict one another, the position of Copernicus and the Bible must be perfectly harmonious."[1]

"Insisting on an earth only a few thousand years old is a big fence around the Cross. . . . It makes me wonder how many people in our culture have been kept away because of it."

To Galileo, truth was not divisible, with science and faith containing conflicting sets of truth. If truth is not divisible, then there is much at stake here. If the Genesis claims are true, and this universe was created by a supernatural being, then this truth must be evident in a scientific examination of the universe. God will be evident in His creation. Yet, if the Genesis account of Creation is faulty, then I face the terrifying possibility that other parts of the Bible may be wrong too. If science is true and my faith is a fraud, then I live in a universe that is a random event. The love I have for my daughters is only meaningful for the eyeblink of years that I am alive as assembled stardust. If my faith is a deception, then the bleak truth is that death will destroy this love.

> *If the Genesis claims are true, and this universe was created by a supernatural being, then this truth must be evident in a scientific examination of the universe. God will be evident in His creation.*

I look at my daughters, and I know which of the two alternatives I desperately wish to be true: that my love for them will endure beyond this life.

But can I believe it?

For some people, faith is enough to overcome the apparently difficult questions that science presents. In an apparent conflict between the truths of Genesis and the truths of science, they are able to ignore or reject scientific truths and march forward with faith alone. Some march humbly. I envy and admire their quiet certainty. Some march with pride and defiance, telling the world that they are right and the rest of the world is wrong, that faith should ignore reason if reason presents difficulties to faith.

(Among all the species on this earth, humans have the unique ability to reason. If we were created in the image of God, then isn't the ability to reason part of His nature? Is rejecting this ability any different from choosing to throw away the gift of vision by wearing a blindfold?)

Ultimately, however, I think it comes down to much, much

more than an individual decision that faith can or should ignore the evidence of science. We live in the twenty-first century, a cultural period that almost worships science. And the questions science raises about Genesis are inescapable. Even if one's faith is strong enough to overcome the questions and doubts that science seems to elicit about Genesis, can one assume that the faith of others is strong enough? Should we tell our friends and coworkers who are beginning to seek God to ignore modern science and take everything on faith? Or should we accept the reality that, at times, faith may not be enough on its own to adequately answer their queries? If our friends—or our children—reject what the Bible teaches because they cannot get past an apparent conflict between science and Genesis, how will we see them in heaven?

Ussher's Estimate

Misguided defenders of faith—both religious leaders and laypeople—who stray onto scientific turf without scientific knowledge, are mocked when easily proven wrong. An example of this is James Ussher, an Irish archbishop who died in 1656.

Ussher, not a scientist by any means, summed the generations listed in the Hebrew Bible. Estimating the reigns of the various rulers and tallying backward, he boldly proclaimed that the world had been created at nightfall preceding October 23, 4004 BC.[2] Ussher used the Bible as a scientific tool to calculate a six-thousand-year-old universe. His claim is often scorned today, with the implication that his

> *With new astronomical evidence in the last forty years, the Genesis claim to a beginning point of the universe has been dramatically validated.*

estimate is representative of the divide between "true" science and "foolish" religion.

Scorners, however, should keep in mind that until widespread acceptance of the big bang theory a few decades ago, the majority of astronomers and physicists believed in an infinitely old, steady state universe. With new astronomical evidence in the last forty years, the Genesis claim to a beginning point of the universe has been dramatically validated.

While the six-thousand-year theory declared by Ussher is drastically different from the now estimated fifteen- to eighteen-billion-year age of the universe, it's still infinitely closer to correct than what most scientists believed until near the end of the twentieth century.

Science as an Ally

One of the foundations of today's Western culture is naturalistic science based on estimating the earth's age of 5 billion years. My daughters will grow up among a sizable percentage of people who believe ours is a random universe, a belief often accepted without examining how the science behind it actually points to a different conclusion.

Let's set aside the question of whether we live on a young or an old earth and focus on an undeniable consequence of living in this culture: any creationist who advocates a young-earth view will have considerable difficulty persuading most listeners outside of his or her church circles that there is a Creator.

Yet something is possible today that was not possible forty years ago. The sword of science that once attacked faith can now be used to defend it. Because so much emphasis is placed on scientific evidence, any Creation explanation that uses this data to point toward God has considerable credibility. That's why this book makes a case for reconciling Genesis with science by supporting the view that the created universe is billions of years old. If you want to share your faith, understanding science as an ally will help tremendously.

I did not ask my friend Jeff to change his mind about his young-earth view. Nor will I ask any other committed Christian to do so. However, I beg any reader with strong belief in a young earth to at least learn the arguments for an older earth and how they harmonize with modern cosmology.

> *If you want to share your faith, understanding science as an ally will help tremendously.*

You need this understanding, if for no other reason than to help that *one* skeptical teenager or cynical adult who makes an eternal decision about a relationship with God based on how effectively *you* present the marriage of Genesis and science. In today's culture, an old-earth viewpoint has a much better chance of convincing someone without faith that we live in a created universe.

But the Bible's Creation account in Genesis is a stepping-stone to a much more important topic—*why* God created this world. If an old-earth stance makes it easier for someone to continue seeking God, then for heaven's sake—and I mean this literally—set aside the dating of the earth as an issue, and please help that broken person in need of a relationship with God. It could be a friend, a coworker. It may be the ones you love most, your children or grandchildren, who are bewildered at how the claims of media and public school contradict their faith. You'll never regret knowing how modern science can now be used as a vigorous defense against their doubts.

All Things to All People

The apostle Paul once said he would be all things to all people in his efforts to share the gospel. He spoke like a Jew to Jews and like a Greek to the Greeks (1 Cor. 9:19–23). We are in a culture of modern science, and we need to speak the language of modern science to reach this audience. I'm confident that Paul would approve of the young earth advocate who is willing to also put the old-earth viewpoint on the table for the sake of someone genuinely seeking faith. At the very least, there is fairness in this, as both points of view are held to be part of orthodox Christian faith.

If this surprises you, you may be pleased to learn the perspective of the Westminster Theological Seminary, one of the largest and most conservative evangelical seminaries in North America:

> Committed as the Seminary is to the inerrancy of Scripture and standing in the Augustinian and Reformed theological tradition, the precise chronological duration of the six days of creation has never been regarded by the Seminary's Board or Faculty as a matter on which *the Scriptures themselves* speak with decisive clarity. The Seminary has always held that an exegetical judgement on this precise issue has never of itself been regarded as a test of Christian orthodoxy or confessional fidelity, until some have sought to make it such in the modern period. In effect, to hold such a position would be to disenfranchise from Augustinian and Reformed orthodoxy some who have, in fact, by God's grace, served as its greatest defenders and pillars.[3]

Yeah, I had to read it more than a couple of times too. Here's my best shot at what it means for a non seminary guy like me: The Seminary is dedicated to understanding divine Scripture and asserts that the Scripture doesn't make clear how precisely it measures the length of days of Creation. Because of this, a believer's view on this chronology is not a test of orthodoxy. While it has never been an issue until now, those who assert that one position or another is such a test are disagreeing with some of the greatest believers in history.

I wish this generosity of reconciliation between differing views was more widely known, and I have Hugh Ross, author of *A Matter of Days*,[4] to thank for making me aware of the Westminster Seminary statement.

In short, there is no dishonesty in allowing or presenting an old-earth view even if you hold a young-earth view. Nor is there reason for mean-spirited debate that tries to force one side to admit the other is correct. Orthodox Christianity makes room for *both* views.

With this in mind, it's too bad—actually tragic, in the truest sense—that former presidential candidate William Jennings Bryan didn't understand the danger of dogmatically insisting on his view, at the worst of times and in the most public of places.

You may have heard of the "Monkey Trial," where Bryan joined the ranks of Christians who built a fence around the Cross. His contribution to this fence was so effective that more than eighty years later, the memory still forms a barrier. But, as with Galileo's story, once you know the whole account, you'll understand that despite wide public perception, the God of Genesis did not lose to modern science.

The Monkey Trial

If Galileo's fight with the Catholic Church marked the beginning of science's triumph over religion, a much more recent trial served, in the public eye, as a final coronation of the victor.

Dayton, Tennessee, 1924: A lawyer and former presidential candidate on one side. A famous criminal lawyer on the other. A high school teacher in the middle.

Evolution versus the Bible. Reason against faith.

The Monkey Trial.

Along with the televised spectacle of O. J. Simpson's murder trial, the Scopes trial is one of the most famous and controversial American legal battles of the twentieth century.

Tennessee, among other states, had passed a law banning the teaching of the relatively new theory of evolution. John Thomas Scopes, a high school biology teacher, was charged with breaking the law by discussing the theory in his classroom. The case might have passed into obscurity except for the involvement of the American Civil Liberties Union, which challenged the law as a violation of the principle of the separation of church and state. What raised the stakes even higher was the participation of William Jennings Bryan, who aided the prosecution, and Clarence Darrow, who defended Scopes.

For the media, it was the perfect circus event, not only a showdown between religion and science but also a face-off between two high-profile figures. Bryan, a well-known lecturer who had run for president three times, was not a trained theologian but a layperson who loved the Bible and believed that Darwinism was a danger to the foundations of morality. Darrow, the most famous American lawyer of the early 1900s, was known worldwide as a brilliant criminal defender, and he believed strongly in the right to teach evolution.

Technically, Darrow could mount no defense. The issue was not whether the law was wrong or evolution was right. His client, Scopes, had broken the law that forbade him to teach evolution. There was no denying that Scopes had taught the concept to his students. Darrow knew this and planned his defense accordingly.

The impact of the trial on public consciousness, then and now, resulted from Darrow's canny move to challenge Bryan to take the stand as a witness on behalf of the Bible's view of Creation. When Bryan foolishly accepted, Darrow succeeded in moving the focus of the trial to an area that no amount of debate has definitively settled—the truth of evolution versus creationism.

Bryan would have done well to decline Darrow's challenge and heed that centuries-old saying of Maimonides: "Conflicts between science and the Bible result from a lack of scientific knowledge or a defective understanding of the Bible."[5]

Bryan was both hampered by a lack of scientific knowledge and in need of a more comprehensive understanding of the Bible. Furthermore, in Darrow, he faced one of the world's foremost trial lawyers, a lawyer intent upon humiliating Bryan with word games, unanswerable questions, and the apparent contradictions of the Genesis account.

Here is one of the exchanges that came as Bryan tried to respond to Darrow's interrogation about the first days of Creation in Genesis:

DARROW. Have you any idea of the length of these periods?

BRYAN. No; I don't.

DARROW. Do you think the sun was made on the fourth day?

BRYAN. Yes.

DARROW. And they had evening and morning without the sun?

BRYAN. I am simply saying it is a period.

DARROW. They had evening and morning for four periods without the sun, do you think?

BRYAN. I believe in creation as there told, and if I am not
   able to explain it, I will accept it.[6]

Imagine your glee—or disgust—as a reporter watching a former
presidential candidate skewered on the witness stand. Few newspapers were as kind in reporting the trial as Memphis, Tennessee's
Commercial Appeal, which published an article that concluded, "It
was not a contest. Consequently there was no victory. Darrow succeeded in showing that Bryan knows little about the science of the
world. Bryan succeeded in bearing witness bravely to the faith which
he believes transcends all the learning of men."[7]

It was such a debacle that Bryan was not allowed on the witness stand the next day. The judge went as far as ordering Bryan's
testimony expunged from the record, giving this ruling: "I feel
that the testimony of Mr. Bryan can shed no light upon any issue
that will be pending before a higher court; the issue now is
whether or not Mr. Scopes taught that man descended from a
lower order of animals."[8]

To make all this more dramatic, and searing it further into
public consciousness, William Jennings Bryan died a few days
later in Dayton while resting after the trial.

The judge, of course, was correct. The trial was not about the
veracity of evolution but about a teacher who had broken a law
that banned teaching it. Darrow lost the trial. Scopes was found
guilty of teaching the theory of evolution. But like Galileo's trial,
it was a Pyrrhic victory. The cultural result was much more far-
reaching. Because Darrow had shifted the focus to a debate against
a badly prepared and overconfident opponent, evolution, as represented by Darrow, came out the victor. Creationism, as represented
by William Jennings Bryan, had no chance on the witness stand,

in court, or in the media, which portrayed all creationists as ignorant and badly out of touch with mainstream science.

Common Misconceptions

Some things haven't changed, huh?

The biggest impact in public consciousness, however, came from a wildly inaccurate retelling of the trial, a play called *Inherit the Wind*, which opened on Broadway in 1955. Even though the playwrights cautioned that they were not pretending to be journalists and the play was also written as a response to McCarthyism, the caricatures they painted of the trial's participants endured in public memory.

In the play, the schoolteacher is dragged out of his classroom and into jail by a mob; in real life, Scopes never faced jail. The people of Dayton were polite, and it was the defense, not the prosecution, who insisted on taking the case to trial. Further, in the theatrical production, Bryan's character, Brady, is transformed into a mindless reactionary. His lines, purported to represent creationist thought, make him sound far more foolish than he did in real life. He opens his defense by insisting that God created the cosmos in six twenty-four-hour days, beginning "on the 23rd of October in the year 4004 BC at—uh, 9:00 a.m.!"[9]

This dramatic piece, in its time, was the longest-running drama on Broadway. Then, in 1960, it became a hit movie starring Spencer Tracy and Gene Kelly. Inaccurate as it was historically, the movie version of *Inherit the Wind* became a popular teaching tool in classrooms.

Because most Americans learned about the trial from stage and screen, the impact of *Inherit the Wind* was far greater than that of the trial itself. Carl Sagan, who to millions represented science because of his television stature, said this: "The movie *Inherit the Wind* probably had a considerable national influence; it was the first time . . . that American movies made explicit the apparent contradictions and inconsistencies in the book of Genesis."[10]

In the public's perception, this impression has not changed in the decades since. It's one of the reasons why introducing intelligent design[11] as a curriculum companion to evolutionary science is such an uphill battle. (Another reason, I believe is

> *Creationism did not lose at the Scopes trial. Only the person who represented it did.*

that the term *intelligent design* has become as polarizing and provocative as the term *evolution*; using it without first defining it makes for heated debate.) The truth that must be emphasized, however, is that creationism did not lose at the Scopes trial. Only the person who represented it did.

Prepare to Be Challenged

While William Jennings Bryan did bear "witness bravely to the faith which he believe[d] transcends all the learning of men,"[12] the hard truth is that he accepted a challenge he could not meet, and his failure has had severe repercussions.

The lesson to be learned from Bryan's failure is simple. Any person with faith in the God of Genesis will see that faith challenged. Maybe in scorn. Maybe as a legitimate question from a truth seeker. Maybe from someone who wants to be reassured. Or maybe by internal doubt.

Be prepared, not overconfident. If you avoid misunderstandings both of the Bible and science, then, when challenged, you will succeed where Bryan failed.

It will also help to understand how we have reached an age in which it often appears that science points to a universe without God. We'll discuss that in the next chapter.

TEN

Man Without God

First scene, outdoors at night:

> CALVIN. *Look at all the stars! The universe just goes out forever and forever!*

> HOBBES. *It kind of makes you wonder why man considers himself such a screaming big deal.*

Following scene, indoors, as Calvin sits in a comfortable chair and points a remote at the television:

> CALVIN TO HOBBES. *That's why we stay inside with our appliances.*

—BILL WATTERSON, *Calvin and Hobbes*

On one of our nature walks, Olivia, Savannah, and I stopped and squatted to watch a vicious death match between a dragonfly and a wasp at our feet. We were fascinated by the horror of it. I was struck by how alien these creatures would have seemed if they were the size of humans: aliens equipped with different weapons. The dragonfly had the size advantage as well as long, dexterous legs, but it had only its mandibles to attack and defend. The wasp had a reservoir of poison and a stinger to pierce the dragonfly's long, vulnerable body.

Had the dragonfly picked the wasp out of the air as it swooped overhead? Had the wasp's struggle forced both of them into a plummet that their external skeletons survived?

However this battle had begun, when we arrived, the dragonfly was on top, using four of its legs to pin the wasp. The wasp was frantically trying to bend its lower body at an angle that would allow it to sting the dragonfly, while the dragonfly arched to avoid the sting. Both creatures' wings flexed against the ground as they wrestled.

This silent struggle, so insignificant to the rest of the world, took at least a minute. Finally the dragonfly managed to sever the head of the wasp from its body, so that the stinger was no longer a threat. After a moment's rest, the dragonfly grappled with the wasp's body, lifted it, and with its long, clear wings undamaged by all the flexing, flew away.

The scene was breathtaking in a macabre way. I've wondered about it a lot since. How did the dragonfly know that the wasp's stinger was a danger? How did it recognize that the way to kill the wasp was to remove its head? From whom did it learn that the wasp was a source of food, and that its bodily liquids would help the dragonfly grow?

Pointless questions, maybe, because I'm forced to relate to the dragonfly from a human perspective. I learn by experience, either from doing or watching. I learn because I'm taught by others. I learn because I can infer and deduct.

With a brain roughly the size of the tip of a pin, how is a dragonfly taught? How does it have the intelligence to make inferences or deductions?

The simplest answer is instinct. But for me, that answer only leads to more questions. What exactly is instinct? How is it written into the DNA of a dragonfly? How can instinct be so specific that a dragonfly knows how to search for food, avoid danger, and reproduce?

Could something as complicated as a dragonfly, with its bulging eyes and gossamer wings, be the product of a random universe, brought into being by strictly naturalistic means? Could the food chain that surrounds it—such an amazingly delicate balancing act that any one domino falling sends the others into chaos—be another happenstance act?

More frightening are the questions that arise if this isn't a naturalistic universe. How can I comprehend the awesome wonder of God the Creator bringing the dragonfly into existence and, among the millions of species, giving it a niche in the world around it? How can I comprehend that a Being with such power has a place for me? Why would He allow me to contemplate His existence and wonder about my purpose?

And if this God is the God of the Bible, how and why is it that He has promised to love me? What is my role and relationship with Him?

What, then, of the mystery of the Cross?

Most of all, how do I help others understand this God of Scripture and His promise of the Cross?

The New God-Is-Dead Era

Cartoonist Bill Watterson's commentary on modern America at the beginning of this chapter offers a wry implication that science without God leads to cynicism and a sense of life without meaning. It wasn't always like this.

Pre-Renaissance mankind held all of nature in superstitious awe. "The gods" spoke during thunderstorms. An eclipse of the sun was a sign from God. Plagues were divinely sent to punish. Poets, artists, and scientists searched without embarrassment for the Creator who gave them life, and they marveled at the awareness of His existence.

Mankind shared the same wonder at the universe that Calvin blurts out to his friend Hobbes: "Look at all the stars! The universe just goes out forever and forever!"

> Into a void without God came naturalism, the dominant worldview in Western culture today.

Then came the European Renaissance, and the wonder began to fade. The church lost its stranglehold on truth; religion—at first gradually, and then cataclysmically—lost its grip on science and art. Mysteries of nature that religion had attributed to the divine seemed suddenly to have simple mechanical explanations. We learned about the behavior of electricity, predicted the effects of gravity and the motions of the planets and stars, understood bacteria, and probed the composition of atoms and molecules.

Earth lost its place at the center of the universe, as did the sun, and, eventually, man. We began to believe that the sunset on the horizon resulted from a mechanical, impersonal, and random universe. For society at large, God became irrelevant, to the point at which a famous late-twentieth-century *Time* magazine cover quizzed, in bold red letters "Is God Dead?"[1]

Into a void without God came naturalism, the dominant worldview in Western culture today.

Man Without God? No "Screaming Big Deal"

Random universe? Or designed?

As mankind's scientific knowledge increased dramatically, an immense divide grew between science and faith. The more we understood about science, the more it seemed unnecessary to include God as part of the clockwork process running the cosmos. It seemed increasingly difficult to hold on to faith in God against the claims of science.

In naturalism, it seemed that the laws of the universe gave simple, natural explanations for how things work. The explanation for our existence could be found in science alone. We are here, the naturalistic community told us, just because. This naturalism was in direct contradiction to the supernatural claims of the Bible. For people whose worldview valued only intellect and reason, nature just existed. Without God. The myths of religious faith were manufactured to comfort people of lesser intelligence.

This was and is the divide.

Widely known author and lecturer Charles Colson, who magnificently applied rational thought to the validity of a Christian worldview in his book *How Now Shall We Live?* expressed it this way:

Naturalism begins with the fundamental assumption that the forces of nature alone are adequate to explain everything that exists. . . . Naturalists say that in the beginning were the particles, along with blind, purposeless natural laws. That nature created the universe out of nothing, through a quantum fluctuation. That nature formed our planet, with its unique ability to support life. That nature drew together the chemicals that formed the first living cell. And naturalism says that nature acted through Darwinian mechanisms to evolve complex life-forms and, finally, human beings, with the marvels of consciousness and intelligence.[2]

Without God in nature, then, against the vastness of an impersonal universe, man has no more or less meaning than a rock or a tree. Thus Hobbes sums up the destination that seemed to wait at the end of the journey that Galileo started: "It kind of makes you wonder why man considers himself such a screaming big deal."

A Knowledge Explosion

In the early 1990s, although some geneticists disagreed, others predicted that within twenty or thirty years, it just might be possible to clone a mammal. Enthralled, I began to read as much as I could about genetics, intrigued by some of the fascinating possibilities for potential novels. Soon, armed with what I had learned, I wrote one of the first speculative novels on the subject. *Double Helix*, a tale of a scientist who tries to clone humans, used fiction to explore some of the real-life implications of DNA research.

But two years—not twenty or thirty—after *Double Helix* was published, I was astounded to read headlines announcing that a Scottish scientist had just introduced Dolly the sheep to the world. Cloning had arrived.

While I am grateful for Dolly—thanks to her, *Double Helix* briefly resurfaced on a best-seller list—I was both indignant and amused four years after publication of *Double Helix* when I saw an Amazon.com reader's review refer to the novel as an "unsophisticated and over-worn plot regarding human cloning."[3] In less than a decade, cloning had gone from science fiction to science fact to science cliché.

The acceleration of accumulated knowledge that began with the cultural paradigm shift of the Renaissance is staggering. And applied technology has accelerated right along with that knowledge.

For the first ten thousand years of recorded human history, the fastest any human could travel was at the speed of a galloping horse—unless he wanted to jump off a cliff. It has only been in the last hundred years or so—that is, in the last two or three generations, a mere blink of time—that technology has allowed us to travel much faster. Some cars can now go at speeds greater than two hundred miles per hour. Airplanes can fly faster than sound. A journey that took the early American settlers weeks or months by wagon over dangerous territory can be accomplished in mere hours on an interstate in air-conditioned comfort.

In fact, thanks to science and technology, most of us truly live better than kings did only one hundred years ago. We live in climate-controlled homes with running water, televisions, and washers and dryers. Doctors no longer routinely try to cure us by applying leeches to suck blood from our bodies; we can get the best of modern drugs and surgeries. We're protected by electronic security systems and advanced military technology; we don't lie awake at night, worrying about barbarians tearing down our towns. We store our wealth in electronic binary codes in bank computers, not in piles of gold or silver that armies can steal.

And technological advances are happening faster and faster. Fewer than forty years ago, man first stepped on the moon; now sport-utility vehicles boast more technology than the early spaceships, and your desktop computer has more calculating power than the computers that placed men in space. With cell phones and laptops, you can instantly communicate via satellite to locations anywhere in the world.

Color TVs first became common only forty-five years ago. Now you can entertain yourself with the virtual reality of music videos, computer games, world news in real time, and theater screens three stories tall.

With this rush of knowledge, we've conquered nature by insulating ourselves against it and by believing we understand it—well, except for a few loose ends. The only relevance nature has in our daily lives is what's forecast on the Weather Channel. The night sky, like a magician's trick explained, has seemingly lost its wonder. It is only natural (pun intended), then, that Calvin replies to Hobbes, "That's why we stay inside with our appliances."

There is a paradox here. On one side, we smugly insulate ourselves from the natural world and focus on becoming the center of our tiny universes, ruling nature in ways that would have astounded people who lived only a hundred years earlier. On the other side, a cynical disbelief in the existence of God prevents us from possibly making the claim that we belong at the center—without God, humans have no more importance than dirt.

In 1935, influential philosopher, mathematician, and outspoken atheist Bertrand Russell summed up the attitude of twentieth-century intellectuals with this statement in his classic book *Religion and Science*: "Before the Copernican revolution, it was natural to suppose that God's purposes were specifically concerned with the earth, but now this has become an implausible hypothesis."[4]

Everything in science to that point suggested his conclusion was inarguable. At the subatomic level, classic nuclear physics had explained the mysteries of the atom. At the cosmic level, Einstein's theory of relativity was expanding Newton's mechanical explanation of the workings of the universe. And on a planetary level, Darwin had explained the existence and development of life. Some even declared that science had neared the end of its journey. What more was there to know?

That was 1935. Russell, like his contemporaries, had no inkling that God was on the horizon. In the next decades, quantum physics succeeded in replacing many of the cherished truths of classic nuclear physics and ushering in new mysteries: atoms were particles and waves at the same time; matter could flicker in and out of existence. Experimental work on Einstein's theories brought as many questions as it answered. And mainstream biologists began to see that patterns in the fossil record did not match the predictions of Darwinism.

Then came the staggering proof that the universe had a beginning. With widespread acceptance of the big bang theory and a universe with a definite starting point, the Genesis view of a created universe suddenly had substance. Science was opening the door to the existence of God again.

So why is it still difficult for Western culture to see God behind the science of this universe?

Some of the blame goes to the media (which usually gets the blame for most of our evils—and despite this becomes more pervasive each year). Conflict sells. Harmony doesn't. The fringes of both science and religion get the most press. The result? We see extreme fundamentalists disagreeing with out-of-the-box science in news clips of thirty seconds or fewer. As a result, today's pop culture finds it difficult to understand good faith or good science—or a reconciliation of the two.

But two much more mundane targets, I believe, should shoulder more of the blame than the media: today's high school science curriculum, and the science remembered by parents ages forty or older.

In both generations—then and now—accumulation of a student's scientific knowledge typically ends at grade 12. When we parents were that age, we probably didn't care about or understand much anyway. (Admit it: you thought you had much better things to do at that time of your life.) Further, although science has shown notable evidence pointing to a supernatural being's involvement in the universe, exceptional high school science teachers with a passion for scientific knowledge beyond what is required are still handcuffed by the curriculum they have no choice but to teach. And *handcuffed* is an accurate term. Today's high school science is further hindered by a factor that wasn't as prevalent thirty or even twenty years ago. In this millennium, our accumulation of knowledge is so rapidly accelerating that a textbook is out-of-date as soon as the ink dries on its pages. That's presuming that those who select the curriculum are even concerned that textbooks bring new science to the classrooms. That would be based on a further presumption that students would be given time to learn classic nineteenth- and twentieth-century science as a foundation to understanding new science and the questions that arise from it. And all of this would be based on the assumption that questions about God that arise from new science would be allowed back into public-school classrooms.

All of these factors make it unlikely that graduating seniors in this generation will learn from science how much of it can point to the existence of God.

The more subtle but equally profound factor is the high school science that all of us over the age of forty remember. There is so much more than the classic nuclear physics, Newton's mechanical view of the universe, and Darwin's theory of evolution that we were taught. Unless we've made an effort to stay up-to-date, our scientific knowledge base as a generation is deficient.

I graduated from high school in 1976—pre-Internet, pre-cell phone, and, yes, even pre-calculator; I did physics calculations using a slide rule. If your background is like mine, as a parent struggling with science versus Genesis, you are hampered by the same scientific limitations that Bertrand Russell faced in 1935, when he declared God's purpose with Earth as an "unplausible hypothesis."

> Today's science is not unfriendly to a created universe.

In short, the high school science that was unfriendly to God in my generation is there to haunt us as parents. Here might be a good place to repeat Francis Bacon's observation: a little science estranges a man from God, but a lot of science brings Him back. The last few decades in science have brought us much, much closer to God. All we have to do is learn more about science to understand the truth in Bacon's statement and the foolishness in Russell's premature conclusion.

Today's science is not unfriendly to a created universe.

In his book *The Science of God*, distinguished physicist and biblical scholar Gerald Schroeder points out that if you avoid a subjective bending of the Bible to match science, or of science to match the Bible, science becomes a strong ally of faith.[5]

As noted in chapter 9, the medieval philosopher Maimonides wrote that conflicts between science and the Bible result from one of two things: a lack of scientific knowledge or a defective understanding of the Bible.[6]

You may be ready to acknowledge that you lack scientific knowledge. But what about your biblical knowledge?

ELEVEN

Misunderstandings of the Bible

Sincere Christians can disagree about the details of
Scripture and theology—absolutely.

—BILLY GRAHAM

For Savannah and Olivia, one of the most compelling stories in
our children's Bible is described in the second chapter of Mark,
where Jesus heals a paralytic.

It has a tremendous emotional impact on them because they
are so easily able to project themselves into the situation, and are
thrilled and amazed at the dramatic miracle. When I start reading
it aloud, my little girls immediately understand that four friends
want to help a fifth, but are unable to reach the man with the
power and love to heal him. They can relate to the frustration of
trying to get through the crowd that prevents them from getting
inside the house where the Healer is.

But when we reach the point in the story where the four
young men lower their buddy through the roof, I am interrupted
by questions, because Olivia and Savannah understand only the
steeply pitched roof of our house.

"How did they get up there?"

"Weren't they afraid of falling?"

"How did they cut a hole in the roof?"

"Did the snow get into the house?"

"Didn't the daddy who owned the house get mad at them for cutting a hole in it?"

"Did pieces of the roof fall on Jesus and the people inside?"

"Wouldn't it get cold in the house if it was wintertime?"

As parents, with a broader knowledge of biblical times, we understand that the climate was warm and the roof of a house there was flat. It was used in the same way that we use our outdoor decks, and there was likely easy access to the roof by a set of stairs.

Those are easy enough answers for me to supply my daughters while they are small enough to sit in my lap during Bible readings. But when they become teenagers, it might not be that simple. Rightfully so, they could argue that if a Jewish roof in that day was built to serve as a deck, then it would have to be strong enough to hold the weight of an entire family. Wouldn't it be difficult to cut through a roof that strong?

I'll be ready then with more details. The roof of a Jewish house, according to historian Alfred Edersheim, was made of hard-beaten earth or rubble and was paved with brick or stone. This makes sense if it was to serve as an outside living area, where families might spend warm evenings. Otherwise, as Olivia or Savannah might point out, it wouldn't bear the weight. Furthermore, Jewish law of that time dictated a building code of sorts; the roof needed a balustrade at least three feet high. Is it likely that the four men would have been able to hack through the solid roof, or would they have even considered it, given the noise and interruption for the people below?

Given his extensive knowledge of Jewish culture in the time of Jesus, Edersheim concludes that Jesus was not below the main roof of the house but in a covered courtyard, beneath a lighter framework that supported tiles.[1]

This knowledge isn't necessary to understand the essence of the story, namely that the quartet helped their friend meet Jesus, and Jesus healed the man, taking the opportunity to make a strong point to the skeptical religious leaders who witnessed the healing. Yet for Savannah and Olivia, it was and is crucial to explain that roofs were different in Jesus' time. Otherwise, the logistics of cutting a hole in the roof would have made it more difficult for them to believe it happened.

> If you've ever had a discussion with anyone on the meaning of a Bible passage, you know how emotionally charged each side can become when views differ, especially when it relates to interpreting the first and last books of the Bible. The beginning of time. And the end of time.

More critical is this: their doubts in Mark's account of this event would have sown seeds for doubting the other events that Mark describes—including the most important event of all.

The Resurrection.

Factual or Figurative?

If you've ever had a discussion with anyone on the meaning of a Bible passage, you know how emotionally charged each side can become when views differ, especially when it relates to interpreting the first and last books of the Bible. The beginning of time. And the end of time.

How literally are we to take Genesis and Revelation? In a cover story for *Newsweek* magazine, Billy Graham said that he went from "seeing every word of Scripture as literally accurate to believing that parts of the Bible are figurative."[2]

Here's a situation where discussions of the meaning of the Bible can quickly become divisive. Is every word literal, or is Billy Graham correct in saying that some of it is metaphorical?

I've immediately brought the Reverend Billy Graham into this discussion because he has shown this generation a lifetime of faith-driven integrity. He's a man we can trust. If a Christian as respected as Graham, and with a faith as strong, is willing to express this opinion, isn't there room for other believers to suggest the same thing, without having their motives or morality questioned? Don't sincere Christians have the right to discuss this issue openly and without rancor?

As much as my wife, Cindy, and I love and respect each other, our discussion did become heated as we discussed the conclusions of the Westminster Theological Seminary that I mentioned in chapter 9. For too long during the discussion, we were arguing about the conclusions, whether Genesis was literal in all senses or figurative in places. Then I realized something that immediately helped both of us.

The WTS was not trying to show that one side was "true" over the other. Instead, the learned scholars came to a consensus that, even with the best of scholarly knowledge of the ancient Hebrew language and culture, they were still unsure of how the text in certain places is to be understood in a twenty-first-century context.

If it looks as though I'm trying to do my best not to offend anyone who may disagree with Billy Graham about the Bible's "figurative" language, you're right. Yet if you still don't like the direction I'm headed, you may want to skip over the next few paragraphs.

Understanding the Bible

No pulled punches here: it takes a substantial amount of either ignorance or arrogance to believe that one can understand the Bible as a newspaper or magazine. One could claim that the Holy Spirit guided him, but how does he answer someone else who claims the same guidance but has a different interpretation?

> It takes a substantial amount of either ignorance or arrogance to believe that one can understand the Bible as a newspaper or magazine.

To avoid misinterpreting the Bible, you must first understand that it is a divinely inspired book, made of a rich tapestry containing many assorted writing genres—poetry, for example. You also need to acknowledge that it was written by a collection of authors from different time periods and diverse cultures to varied audiences in several languages. The most recent writing in the Bible is still nearly two thousand years old. Without an understanding of historical, cultural, genre, and biblical context, many crucial nuances are lost.

I was in a classroom recently, leading a writing workshop for twelve-year-old students at a Christian school, when one of them asked why I had written *The Last Disciple*, the controversial historical novel that I coauthored with Hank Hanegraaff. I asked one of the girls to humor me and tell me where in the world we lived. She began with the continent of North America and narrowed it down from there. I then asked one of the boys to get the globe at the back of the classroom and show the rest of the class the place she meant. He did it without giving it much thought.

I told them that this showed that they thought about their location in terms of the entire globe—such a fundamental premise that none thought it was unusual. At the age of twelve, they were already so entrenched in this global view that they were unable to think about the world in any other way. They've seen pictures of Earth shot from outer space. They're aware that Earth is a planet in the solar system. Television images every day help them realize the diversity and size of Planet Earth. Many of them communicate via the Internet with people in other countries.

Two thousand years ago, I suggested, no person alive would have had that perspective, particularly an unschooled preteen who had never traveled more than five miles from his or her village. In a different time and culture, the connotations behind the word *world* were vastly different. To an author or reader living in the time of Jesus, a simple phrase such as "punishment inflicted on the entire world" would not necessarily mean a global conflict. The "world" might mean the Roman Empire or even an area as local as the land of the Jews, depending on which Hebrew word had been used.

Unfortunately, these types of ingrained cultural presumptions are not the only barrier to a better understanding of the Bible.

The Crisis of Context

"My wife beat me," I told a friend recently. My friend didn't raise an eyebrow.

Seconds earlier, I'd been telling him that Cindy and I had both left the same place at the same time, but in different vehicles and using separate routes.

I'd predicted that I would get me home first. Cindy had disagreed. She was right.

She beat me. By five minutes.

It's amazing how good we are at understanding context, given that so few of our words are unequivocal. That is, one word might have several meanings, depending on how it is used in a sentence, or even how that sentence is used with other sentences around it.

> One word might have several meanings, depending on how it is used in a sentence, or even how that sentence is used with other sentences around it.

"He marches to the *beat* of a different drum." In conversation, you don't stop and consciously give thought to the fact that *beat* is a noun here.

"He picked up the stick and *beat* the snake." Now it's a verb, referring to a striking action. But when I said, "My wife *beat* me," it was a verb with a different meaning.

"I'm *beat*." It's become an adjective.

It isn't hard to understand the context of a word or a sentence of this type if you've been raised with the English language. The difficulty becomes exponential, however, if you're a scholar dealing with an original language two thousand years old in a Middle Eastern culture. Double that difficulty when you're a layperson reading King James English that's been translated from Hebrew and Greek. Double it again when, no matter how deep your faith or pure your motives, you are unaware of the possibility of ambiguous meanings as you read. Or worse, if you know which meaning is right, but you choose the one that suits you better.

How dangerous can this misunderstanding be on a personal level?

In his book *The Apocalypse Code*, author Hank Hanegraaff tells of a famous atheist who discarded his Christian faith during his university days after giving critical thought to Jesus' parable of the mustard seed (Matt. 13:31–32; Mark 4:30–32; Luke 13:18–19). In this parable, Jesus described the mustard seed as the smallest seed in the world. Yet from a scientific and global twenty-first-century perspective, this description is inaccurate. There are smaller seeds. The atheist rejected his faith because he reasoned that if Jesus could not get that fact correct, then He, whether a deliberate or accidental liar, could not be the divine and perfect Son of God.

In a historical context, however, the world of Jesus and His listeners was not the globe that you and I picture when we think of our planet. In a cultural context, a mustard seed as the smallest seed was the most apt and accurate word picture that He could use for the point He was trying to make.

Armed with this knowledge, would you still decide that Jesus was a liar? And give up your faith because of it?

When Jesus walked this earth in a human body, was His tongue the two-edged sword described in Revelation (1:17)? You would have to read the Bible in a wooden, literal sense to argue this, and I doubt anyone would. We would all agree that the description is figurative. And we would all agree, then, that the Bible does use figurative language. But *where* is it figurative, and *where* is it literal? [3]

Ah, there's the rub.

The concern about not accepting liberal interpretations of biblical texts is understandable. After all, there are clearly parts of the Bible that are written as eyewitness accounts of historical events, *including much of the New Testament. For a believer, the events recorded in these sections ought to be taken as the writer intended— as descriptions of observed facts. But other parts of the Bible, such as the first few chapters of Genesis, the book of Job, the Song of Solomon and the Psalms, have a more lyrical and allegorical flavor and do not generally seem to carry the marks of pure historical narrative. . . . Would it have served God's purposes thirty-four hundred years ago to lecture to his people about radioactive decay, geologic strata, and DNA?[4] —Dr. Francis Collins*

Extrabiblical Proofs

Even if you know nothing about golf, you could watch the Masters golf tournament on a black-and-white television with the sound turned off, and you would still know who was in the lead, who was chasing, when the final putt dropped, and, ultimately, who won. Yet seeing it in color would make for a much richer experience. Hearing the commentators discuss the difficulty of a driver or an approach would give you an appreciation for the joy of a spectacular shot or the agony of a missed one. Knowing a player's history, or the history of the tournament or the game, would give you a vital new perspective.

In short, you'd know and understand a lot more about the Masters this way.

Yes, the Bible in black and white clearly delivers its important message meant for twenty-first-century readers, because one of the glories of the Word is that even without understanding all of its historical and cultural context, we can recognize that God created us, loves us, and sent His Son, Jesus, to show us the way to reach Him.

In color—that is, with the help of commentators who give you the cultural and historical context—you can get far more out of your Bible reading.

But may I add a caveat?

Using the Bible to argue science puts you in a bad position, especially when debating another Christian. For example, some make their case for the Genesis account based on the premise that the Bible is true because it's God's Word, and God says it's true. This verges far too close to a fallacy known as *circular reasoning*, "an attempt to support a statement by simply repeating the statement in different or stronger terms."[5]

Don't get me wrong here. I'm not suggesting their assertion is false, but if you're going to step into an argument, formal or not, you are agreeing, implicitly or not, to the rules in this arena. Circular reasoning (also known as "begging the question") is a fallacy, and in logical terms (not faith terms!) their assertion—that the Genesis account is true because it's God's Word, and God's Word is true because the Bible says it's true—is easily defeated in an argument.

On the other hand, if you avoid circular reasoning and look for extrabiblical truths, such as archaeological discoveries, that support the Bible's claims, you will be in safe and comforting territory in the ring of argument. As an example, skeptical scholars once believed that no such figure as Pontius Pilate existed in history—until they found inscriptions of his name during excavations of modern Caesarea.

> *Don't use the Bible to argue science. But use science to argue the Bible, and you won't be defeated.*

Don't use the Bible to argue science. But use science to argue the Bible, and you won't be defeated.

A Slippery Slope

One of the biggest obstacles to reconciling science with Genesis is accepting whether the Creation account in the Bible took place in literal twenty-four-hour days or figurative days. This, then, is one of the most critical areas of biblical understanding—or misunderstanding—when applied to science. With that in mind, I'd like to point out another fallacy in argumentation: the *slippery slope*. It goes like this:

You believe that some of Genesis is not literal, but figurative. Next you'll insist that other parts of the Bible are figurative, and soon you'll be trying to tell me that Jesus was just another teacher.

First, the slippery-slope argument is disrespectful. Life is a progression of valleys and hills. As we mature in our reasoning abilities, we learn how to hold our position on slopes. Second, it is flawed, because the first premise does not necessarily lead to the next. If you insist that describing some parts of the Bible as figurative means that the entire Bible will be painted with the same brush, then you'd better be prepared to also insist that Jesus had a sword for a tongue.

From the *Newsweek* article on Billy Graham:

Now, more than a half a century later, he is far from questioning the fundamentals of faith. He is not saying Jesus is just another lifestyle choice, nor is he backtracking on essentials as the Incarnation or the Atonement. But he is arguing that fair-minded Christians may disagree or come to different conclusions about different points. Like Saint Paul, he believes human beings on this side of paradise can grasp only so much. "Now we see but a poor reflection as in a mirror," Paul wrote, "then we shall see face to face." *Then* believers shall see: not now, but *then*.[6]

I'm taking a deep breath now, because I'd also like to agree with Graham when, as reported in *Newsweek*, he says that the word *day* is possibly figurative in Genesis.[7]

If you don't agree, and if you want to close the book right now or throw it at the wall, I'm pleading, again, that you leave room for fellow believers, and especially your questioning children, to legitimately consider a less literal interpretation within Christian orthodoxy, without the accusation that other parts of the Bible must become figurative too. I'm asking you to consider the day when your inquisitive child, or someone else near you, seeks the Cross, and to realize that allowing room for a differing view might remove a fence in the way.

Why are so many respected Christians, such as the Reverend Billy Graham, willing to concede that the six days of Creation in Genesis *might* be longer than twenty-four hours each?

The ancient Hebrew word for "day" is *yôm*, which has several meanings in biblical Hebrew. In the late 1990s the Presbyterian Church of America convened a panel of scholars "to determine the limits of permissible interpretations of the Genesis 1 Creation days under the assumptions of strict biblical supernaturalism, a denial of naturalistic interpretations of life's history on earth, a belief in creation ex nihilo (out of nothing), and a belief in Adam and Eve as actual historical persons from whom all of humanity is descended."[8]

> *Why are so many respected Christians, such as the Reverend Billy Graham, willing to concede that the six days of Creation in Genesis* might *be longer than twenty-four hours each?*

Two years of deliberation resulted in a ninety-two-page report that agreed with the Westminster Theological Seminary that there are four different views of the Creation days deemed within the bounds of Christian orthodoxy:

> *Calendar day*: Creation days consist of six consecutive twenty-four-hour periods that are historical and chronological.

> *Day-age*: Creation days are six consecutive long ages that are historical, sequential, and chronological.

> *Framework*: the Creation week is a metaphor to narrate God's actions in Creation with the days to be understood as topical rather than sequential and the durations as unspecified.

> *Analogical days*: Creation days are analogous to, but not necessarily identical to, human days, that is, broadly consecutive but of unspecified length.

As further reassurance that believers can consider Genesis from a perspective of an older earth, I was heartened to find the conclusion of noted Hebrew scholar Kenneth A. Mathews in a Bible commentary published by a conservative press affiliated with the Southern Baptist Convention:

"The weight of the arguments favors a nonliteral "day", but definitive answers to the meaning of "day" and the duration of creation remain elusive."[9]

If you are able to consider the six-day Creation account in Genesis as unfolding over six segments of time without reference to solar days, it is breathtaking to realize that the only explanation for the accuracy of the Genesis account is divine inspiration, thousands of years before science could confirm the timing of the events. Remember, from chapter 3, former atheist Antony Flew's remark:

"I am very much impressed with physicist Gerald Schroeder's comments on Genesis 1 [in *The Science of God*]. That this biblical account might be scientifically accurate raises the possibility that it is revelation."

In his book The Science of God, *author Gerald L. Schroeder presents an interesting hypothesis.*

He first notes, "The opening chapter of Genesis acts like the zoom lens of a camera. Day by day it focuses with increasing detail on less and less time and space. The first day of Genesis encompasses the entire universe. By the third day, only earth is discussed. After day six, only that line of humanity leading to the patriarch Abraham is in biblical view. The Bible realizes that the entire universe exists. But its interest now rests solely on one line of humanity. This narrowing of perspective, in which each successive day presents in greater detail a smaller scope of time and space, finds a parallel in scientific notation."[10]

Schroeder, who is an applied theologian with undergraduate and doctoral degrees from the Massachusetts Institute of Technology, goes on to discuss Einstein's theory of relativity, a description of how changes in gravity or changes in velocity affect the rate at which time flows. (If you were traveling at close to the speed of light, for example, two minutes passing for you might take two thousand years to pass for the rest of us on earth.)

Schroeder notes that our earthly perspective looks back from the present and surveys the billions of years it took for the unfolding of Creation. But the Bible's perspective is one that looks forward from the beginning moment of time. Given this premise, and given the demonstrable truth in Einstein's theory, Schroeder makes a good mathematical argument that each perspective supports the other within the first six days of Creation.

Here's how Schroeder shows the parallels that strongly suggest this revelation:

Genesis 1:1–5: God created the universe. Light was separated from the dark.

Science: Creation began with the big bang. Light was literally formed as the universe cooled enough for electrons to bond to nuclei, and radiation could move outward unimpeded.

Genesis 1:6–8: God formed the heavenly firmament.

Science: Gravity caused material to clump together, the galaxies formed, and so did our solar system.

Genesis 1:9–13: God separates land and the oceans; God brought into existence the first plant life on Earth.

Science: As the earth cooled, water allowed the existence of bacteria and algae and subsequent plant life.

Genesis 1:14–19: God caused the sky to show the bright lights of the heavenly bodies.

Science: The atmosphere becomes transparent, and photosynthesis leads to an oxygen-rich atmosphere.

Genesis 1:20–23: God filled the waters and then the air with animal life.

Science: Animals appeared in the oceans; birds appeared above water and land.

Genesis 1:24–25: God called forth the land animals.
Science: From the animals of the ocean came the animals of the land.

Genesis 1:26–27: God created man.
Science: At the pinnacle of all the events that began with the big bang, man appeared in the universe to marvel at it and question its existence.[11]

It has taken the last four centuries and all our modern technology to produce the scientific picture of the order of creation. If not divinely inspired, how did the ancients who gave us Genesis know it so well and so accurately?

Perhaps a better question is this: how has science been able to validate the Genesis account? To get to that answer, first it's important to avoid misunderstanding science.

TWELVE

Misunderstandings of Science

The scientist is possessed by the sense of universal causation. His religious feeling takes the form of a rapturous amazement at the harmony of natural law, which reveals an intelligence of such superiority that, compared with it, all the systematic thinking and acting of human beings is an utterly insignificant reflection.

—ALBERT EINSTEIN

I once had a satisfying—but very temporary—fatherhood moment in the car when Olivia was just learning to put sentences together. Cindy and I were in the front, with Olivia in the back, directly behind Cindy, strapped like a prisoner in her car seat.

The light had changed and I'd begun to accelerate when Olivia spoke with some satisfaction. "Red means go, Daddy." She'd waited for the light to change to state her conclusion, which suggested that she'd been thinking about it and wanted the car to move to give her verification. I liked her early attempt at cause-and-effect thinking. I wasn't especially concerned that she was wrong; learning, after all, often comes from mistakes and, more important, from the willingness to make them.

Watching the road ahead of me, I said, "Boo-Boo"—years

later, she may not appreciate my using her nickname here—"red means stop."

"Red means go."

"Are you trying to tease Daddy? Red means stop."

"Red means go."

"No, Boo-Boo," I said, a model of patience. My satisfaction at her attempt at critical thinking was fading. "Red means stop."

If you've ever dealt with a stubborn young child, you can imagine how little the conversation varied for the next few blocks. *Red means stop. Red means go. Red means stop. Red means go.*

We stopped at the next set of lights. "See," I said, "red means stop."

Silence. Had I convinced her?

No. Seconds later, as if she'd taken the time to look for herself, she said. "Green means stop."

This new twist in the argument continued until the light turned. I accelerated, eyes ahead on traffic. "See," I said, "green means go."

"No, Daddy. Red means go."

Critical Thinking Skills

There's a reason I thought Olivia had been trying to tease me: example is a powerful teacher.

One of my goals as a father is to help my daughters become critical thinkers. I hope I've been doing it right, since there wasn't much in the parenthood guides on how to help toddlers with this.

"Look at the beautiful purple horses," I say as we drive down a country road past some cows.

"Daddy!" Savannah (not yet three) giggles. "Those are cows."

"Are you sure?"

"And they are not purple!" Olivia (a few years older) adds with a degree of indignation. "They are brown."

As I mentioned, I'm not sure if this method should be recommended. But it's important to me that my daughters learn to evaluate what they are told and have the courage to question it and come to their own conclusions.

I realize there is danger in this. I've had to teach them the difference between questioning facts/conclusions and questioning

> It's important to me that my daughters learn to evaluate what they are told and have the courage to question it and come to their own conclusions. I realize there is danger in this.

parental commands. (We're still working on it.) And I've successfully taught them the "Daddy voice," that deep, urgent tone that must be instantly obeyed. (I use it only if the girls are about to put themselves in physical danger.) But I still want them to be courageous enough to challenge what is presented as truth, and I hope they will be respectful when they do, especially when such evidence is being presented by other adults.

I know some adults won't like having their utterances challenged, no matter how much respect is shown. And I expect that my daughters' ability to think critically will be a double-edged sword in our household as they become teenagers. Yet I hope it pays off. My daughters are accustomed to discussing issues with me now. It will be wonderful if that continues when they face peer pressure. And because I can't force them to follow Christ, I pray that my daughters will choose for themselves to place their trust in the Creator of the universe and walk with Him by faith.

A faith that withstands internal and external tests. A faith that withstands pressure.

Like, to some degree, the pressure I exerted on Olivia to change her mind about that red light.

How to Misconstrue: A Mini Lesson

The argument lasted for two weeks. Olivia's stubbornness and patience both impressed and frustrated me. Occasionally I'd be the one to bring the subject up, speaking as we slowed down for a stoplight. "The light is red," I'd say. "Daddy is getting ready to stop."

The vehicle would be settling on its springs, and Olivia would counter, "Green is stop." And, since I was the one to bring up the dispute again, she'd try to get the last word by waiting until the vehicle moved to say, "Red is go."

Cindy, of course, found it all amusing. But my frustration continued to grow.

Finally, at one light, with our vehicle first in line, I turned, leaned back, and stuck my head between the seats to look Olivia directly in the eyes. She was going to get the Daddy voice, and this discussion would be over. Critical thinking was one thing, but a determined effort to remain wrong in the face of reality was another.

"Olivia," I began, as sternly as I could, "red means *stop*."

She looked away from me—out the window, to her right. "Daddy," she said, quietly and sadly, because of my intimidating tone, "green means stop."

That's when I saw the reason for her adamancy: I saw her view of the traffic light—not the light directly ahead of our vehicle, but the one for cross traffic. My light was red, but from her car seat, she couldn't see that. The front passenger seat blocked her view.

Since my light was red, the cross-traffic signal, the only one she could see, was green, the same green she saw whenever we stopped—which would turn red, of course, just before I accelerated through the intersection.

Red means go, Daddy. Green means stop.

Want a quick lesson in how to misunderstand something in a dispute with someone else? Don't establish *definitions*. Don't agree on *parameters*. Make *assumptions*. And most of all, avoid trying to find a *common perspective*.

In the traffic-light dispute with Boo-Boo, Daddy was guilty of all four errors.

Definitions

Olivia is in school now, and her principal is Mr. Barthel. To me, he's Bob. And my perspective on him is different not only from Olivia's but also from that of most of the students' parents.

Bob and I have known each other for thirty years. We were high school friends. We went away to college together. Shared the two-thousand-mile drive from Alberta to Michigan and back every year. Lived in the same dorm room. Played hockey on the college team. I put on a dress and danced at his wedding (long story, but not what you'd think).

Bob is quality, integrity, and thoughtfulness, exactly the man you would want as a principal and leader of your child's school. The only thing I don't like about him is his irritating ability to eat entire cows and metabolize every calorie merely by breathing. Most of us the same age have accumulated a higher percentage of body fat than Bob ever will.

Recently, Bob and I talked science during a social evening when the subject of evolution came up.

If you're looking for a word that is guaranteed to polarize and provoke, *evolution* is at the top of the list. It's difficult to bring up the subject without getting an emotional reaction. People define themselves by their adamant belief or unbelief in it.

But what, exactly, are we talking about when we discuss evolution?

Bob is the principal of a Christian school. It's an unusual situation in that his school is part of the public school district and is offered as an alternative.

During our conversation, he told me that parents of prospective students often sit in his office and ask his views on evolution. He knows it's a test.

They rarely get the response they expect.

"Evolution?" he will say. "What exactly do you mean by *evolution?*"

"Well, evolution."

"Yes," he says, "evolution is change. Are you asking me what I think about the fact that there is change in the world?"

"Animal evolution."

"Animals change through breeding, for example. Is that what you mean?"

"You know, *evolution.*"

"Evolution as a theory that rejects a world created not by God, but by strictly naturalistic forces?"

"Yes. That."

"And what part of my views are you interested in? An examination of the fossil record? Whether it is an established theory? Whether I agree with the theory? How it fits into the science curriculum? Whether we discuss or ignore the theory? Whether it's important for Christian students in the twenty-first century to be aware of the theory?"

By then, of course, Bob has established what needs to be established. Definition. Without it, any response he makes to such an emotionally sensitive issue is not only prone to misinterpretation but is almost *guaranteed* to be misinterpreted.

But he has also established something else that's just as important. Bob has established the parameters.

Parameters

What can science tell us about the nature of God?

Nothing. As we are learning, science can only point to the existence of God, not to why He created the universe, who He is, where He came from, or how we should relate to Him.

Truth may be indivisible, but searching for it is a lot less complicated when science discussions remain in the realm of science, and theology discussions remain in the realm of theology.

Parameters. The Bible is not a science manual.

Some laypeople resist the conclusions of modern cosmic science by disputing the accumulated data of the different disciplines of science. It's a good smoke-and-mirrors trick but not much more. Broadly speaking, one scientist's experimental data, whether it is centuries old or this month's, is not accepted unless other scientists can verify it under similar experimental conditions.

If someone with twenty years of intense study, and equal years' experience with highly specialized instruments, presents a certain collection of data, it's sheer arrogance for a layperson to dispute such data. (How many of *us* have access to the Hubble telescope?)

I don't have the time or knowledge to verify the distance to the sun or the way DNA replicates or the behavior of electrons at a nuclear level as shown in particle accelerators. Scientists can and do verify such things for me. The personal consequences in the scientific world for reporting false data are so severe that it rarely happens. Science is a self-correcting discipline.

However, there is room to dispute the *conclusions* that can be drawn from the data—inarguable data can lead to arguable conclusions. That is why there are often so many disputes in the scientific world; the interpretation of data generates volumes of argument, because data can suggest a variety of conclusions.

In an ideal world, our children would clearly understand this difference as they receive their education. It is unfair for atheistic science teachers to use scientific data to force a naturalistic worldview upon young students too inexperienced to realize that inarguable data can lead to arguable conclusions. Rather, as explained in earlier chapters about the big bang and the highly improbable likelihood that life should exist at all, modern science is hard-pressed to avoid a conclusion about God from the last four centuries of undisputed data. All they're really capable of doing is making assumptions.

> *Inarguable data can lead to arguable conclusions.*

Assumptions

One of the premises of this book is that truth is indivisible. If so, the battle is not between the truths of faith in science and the truth of faith in God, but between worldviews of people who choose only one portion of the truth and then interpret data according to their personal biases.

A studied theologian who assumes that articles in the popular press provide enough knowledge to evaluate the validity of scientific discoveries is as guilty of ignorance as the scientist at the top of his field who assumes that a simple reading of the Bible is enough to acquire biblical wisdom. (In chapter 14, you'll see how Richard Dawkins, in *The God Delusion*, is extremely and maliciously guilty of this.)

With the arrogance of assumed knowledge, meaningful discussion between the sides is impossible, no matter how committed each might be to finding truth, because each lacks respect for the other's perspective.

Perspective

It's important to keep in mind that Genesis was not penned in the twenty-first century. It was not a scientific paper, written for review by a panel of scientists. It was first recounted orally, long before Einstein and other experts gave us the theory of relativity, the big bang theory, and the timeline of cosmology.

Yet even without this scientific knowledge, the ancients simply and elegantly expressed the cosmic truth of our existence in Genesis 2:7: "The LORD God formed a man's body from the dust of the ground . . ." (TLB). Modern cosmology verifies this wisdom from antiquity, and science shows that the fifty-nine elements found in the human body are also present in the earth's crust. About two-thirds of the body is made of oxygen—the most plentiful element on the outermost layer of our planet.

Had the ancients simply stopped by declaring that we are formed from the dust of the ground, no scientist would dispute the worldview of Genesis. But the most profound aspect of human existence lies in the rest of that bold declaration: ". . . and breathed into it the breath of life" (v. 7 TLB).

This is the core issue, the foundation of human existence, upon which every personal philosophy must rest: Are we merely cosmic debris belched forth from the stars, the products of a random universe? Or were we created with souls engineered for union with God in this life and beyond?

The Lord God breathed into this dust the breath of life. Whether this phrase is meant to be interpreted literally or metaphorically, it shines with truth.

Given their understanding of the world around them, and their lack of modern scientific terms, the ancients tell us—in a language of wonderful simplicity and elegance—that God, by some method outside of our perceived laws of nature, created all life, including human life.

The data of modern cosmic science tell us the same thing. It's called the big bang.

PART FOUR
Harmony

Dear Olivia and Savannah,

Many Christians are afraid to study what science says about the big bang, because they're afraid that would be disrespectful to God and would go against the Bible's story of Creation. But there's really no need for Christians to be afraid of the big bang theory. On the other hand, many scientists are afraid of this theory because it forces them to think about God even if they don't want to believe in Him.

And remember when we talked about how important it is for people to understand each other's definitions and viewpoints before trying to have a good conversation? That's very, very important when we talk about the theory of evolution. Where things really go wrong is when people confuse evolution with evolutionism. Evolution is a scientific explanation of how things change, while evolutionism is a belief that puts science in the place of God.

This is a confusing discussion, but it might help to remember that as smart as monkeys and dolphins are, they're nowhere close to humans. We're so far advanced beyond them that there's no question—humans are special.

God gave us the Creation story in Genesis to assure us of how special we are. It reminds us that we are people who are loved by God, designed for His purpose, and blessed with the gift of freedom to make our own choices about what to believe. How exactly we were created is less important than Who created us. We came from God, and now He lovingly draws us back to Himself. And being home with Him together someday is the only thing that really, really matters.

Love,
Your Daddy

In many Christian circles, the big bang theory is a monster in the closet.

It lurks in dark shadows of misunderstanding and seems to be an enemy to belief in the God of Genesis. Worse, because of overwhelming evidence in favor of the big bang theory, it seems to be an enemy that can be defeated only by leaving the closet door closed and finding a way to ignore it long enough to go back to sleep.

But we don't need to "bam" this monster. It's our friend.

A "God Thing"

One indication of how much of a friend we have in the theory starts with understanding how generations of naturalistic scientists reacted to the evidence for it. Dismissively. Disdainfully. Disrespectfully.

The eternal, steady state universe was the reigning cosmological theory through most of the first half of the twentieth century. The big bang theory ran into much resistance in the scientific world. It was not so much the evidence that was resisted but rather the conclusions that were drawn from it. At least one great physicist was honest enough to acknowledge this. Famous in scientific circles, Arthur Eddington called the big bang theory philosophically "repugnant."[1]

Note that.

Philosophy in science. A determined predisposition to resist the idea of God.

Why was the big bang theory so repugnant to some scientists?

In his book *Stephen Hawking's Universe: The Cosmos Explained*, David Filken, a former head of BBC's television science department, observed, "For atheistic scientists who wanted to reject the idea of a universe created by God, it was vital to explain how all the known elements had naturally evolved in this universe. It seemed the most effective way to counter the arguments of the religious creationists."[2]

Without God in the universe, the foundation of naturalistic science is that the evolution of the universe and its life forms resulted from endless and purposeless cause and effect. This is the worldview of naturalism: faith in natural explanations for everything, even if the explanations have not yet been found.

> *This is the worldview of naturalism: faith in natural explanations for everything, even if the explanations have not yet been found.*

An eternal universe fit nicely into this philosophy: no beginning, no God.

Then scientists began to trace cause and effect farther and farther back in time. Much to their dismay, the theory of an eternal universe began to crumble. By the 1960s, as pointed out in earlier chapters, enough evidence had accumulated to make it difficult to deny that the universe indeed had a beginning.

The most troublesome issue to those who, as Filken said, "wanted to reject the idea of a universe created by God" was that, once they had traced and explained every step as far back in time as possible, they finally came to a beginning point outside any scientific explanation. In those first fractions of a second at the beginning of the universe lurked something frightening—at least to a determined atheist. For an almost infinitely small moment, none of the known laws of physics existed. It was only after the universe came into being that physics, as we know it, could be applied to our universe. In short, the investigators discovered that the beginning is the great unknowable, with no way within science to ever answer questions about the very beginning.

Just as frightening to atheists were the other questions raised: Why did this "first cause" happen? How was it caused?

Genesis had the answer a long time ago: it's a God thing.

Importance of the Big Bang

How important, theologically, is the big bang?

Author Charles Colson points out, "Far from supporting naturalism, big bang theory shows the limits of all naturalist accounts by revealing that nature itself—time, space, and matter—came into existence a finite period of time ago."[3]

Atheist cosmologist Stephen Hawking is one of the most famous scientists since Albert Einstein, and he indirectly agrees with Charles Colson: "Many people do not like the idea that time has a beginning, probably because it smacks of divine intervention."[4] The universe had a beginning. Those who trust the Genesis account have known that for centuries.

In 1981 the Vatican sponsored an international conference on scientific cosmology. It was a shrewd public relations move, given the bad rap that has followed the church since it dealt so shabbily with Galileo. It also showed that the church sensed the shift caused by new cosmic evidence and was back on safe ground when it came to deism in science.

Pope John Paul II took good advantage of this. He made this statement to the assembly of physicists who represented the finest scientific minds in the world, a statement against which they were hard-pressed to successfully argue:

Any scientific hypothesis on the origin of the world, such as that of a primeval atom from which the whole of the physical world derived, leaves open the problem concerning the beginning of the Universe. Science cannot by itself resolve such a question: what is needed is that human knowledge that rises above physics and astrophysics and which is called metaphysics; it needs above all the knowledge that comes from the revelation of God.[5]

Between the lines, Pope John Paul II was also saying something else: all the incredible scientific progress that had continued after Galileo had made possible a reconciliation of faith and science in the minds of believers.

If so much evidence points to a beginning point in time and space that comes from outside nature—the supernatural—then why does much of the mainstream scientific community apparently resist the notion of God? Why, for example, did Eddington react to early big bang theory and its implications of a Creator as he did, calling it philosophically "repugnant"? No one, of course, can answer for an individual scientist except for that scientist, so the only guesses I can make are general.

Many scientists serve in their churches as well as in their laboratories, and I applaud their faithfulness in enduring criticism from both naturalistic colleagues and misguided Christians.

But before I go into that, is it necessarily true that mainstream science is so resistant? Many scientists do, as the quotes in this book show, acknowledge at least the possibility of a supernatural Creator. In fact, many scientists serve in their churches as well as in their laboratories, and I applaud their faithfulness in enduring criticism from both naturalistic colleagues and misguided Christians. I hope this book makes their lives easier as more believers learn how faith and science can find harmony in explaining our origins.

Among scientists who do oppose the idea of God, one reason is that evidence may *suggest* a supernatural Creator, but nothing can—at least within science's present boundaries—empirically *prove* His existence. Some scientists may find it difficult, as do many outside of science, to have faith in something that cannot be quantified, especially because of the theological questions beyond the scope of science: Why is there evil in the world? How has God presented Himself to humankind? Is there an afterlife?

Another reason is simply pride. If God created humankind, then we are lesser beings. The notion of not being in ultimate control of human destiny, despite all we have accomplished through science and technology, is humbling. Even if someone—whether scientist, artist, tradesman, or other—is willing to accept a vague supernatural force in the universe, pride may prevent that person from accepting the God of Genesis, who clearly asserts His supremacy.

Stephen Hawking touched on another reason when he referred to the religious aspect that comes with pursuit of Creation. Look back on the shambles of history and survey—among the shining examples of faith that reflect the love of God—the grief that man-made distortions of religion have brought upon humankind, such as the Inquisition, the Crusades, and 9/11, in the name of "God." Is it any wonder that so many people try to avoid religious disputes?

Days of Creation

What is the major difficulty some Christian readers of Genesis have with the big bang theory?

We're back to the issue of six days of Creation.

If Genesis tells us the entire universe was created in one hundred forty-four hours and is only thousands of years old, there is no room for science and the overwhelming data that lead to the conclusions of the big bang theory. For a creationist who insists on supporting the young-earth interpretation of Genesis, the big bang is an unfriendly monster in a closet.

Yet if a day in Genesis (*yôm*) is understood as a segment of time without reference to solar days, then the big bang theory shows how God used epochs measured in millions and billions of years to create a world for humans. For an old-earth creationist, Genesis and science mesh in a dance of elegance and breathtaking truth.

Without God, how do you explain from the mathematically impossible coincidences in the data behind the anthropic principle that the laws of physics so perfectly allowed a fifteen- to eighteen-billion-year process of creating life? How do you explain the moment when the universe first burst into time and space from nothing?

And always that pesky question: why?

In a naturalistic universe—one that is random and without God—the *why* is explained very simply: because that's the way it is. The challenge for an atheistic scientist, then, is to prove that this is a purposeless naturalistic universe against the scientific evidence that suggests a supernatural Creator.

Patrick Glynn, author of *God: The Evidence*, hits the nail on the head when he says, "Many scientists are profoundly uncomfortable with the universe of the new cosmology, precisely because it leaves ample room for God. The whole picture is damnably disconcerting: a universe with a beginning, designed for man. Many scientists want this picture to go away."[6]

At the Vatican-sponsored conference on scientific cosmology in 1981, cosmologist Stephen Hawking was in the audience listening to Pope John Paul II's opening statement. Indirectly, Hawking had no choice but to agree, as shown by what he later wrote in his *New York Times* best seller *A Brief History of Time*: "So long as the universe had a beginning, we could suppose it had a creator. But if the universe is really completely self-contained, having no boundary or edge, it would have neither beginning nor end: It would simply be. What place then, for a creator?"[7]

> The challenge for an atheistic scientist, then, is to prove that this is a purposeless naturalistic universe against the scientific evidence that suggests a supernatural Creator.

The first half of this quote shows the immense difficulty that nondeistic science has with a definite beginning to the universe. The best in science have no choice but to agree: if the universe had a beginning, then a beginning point makes room for the possibility of God.

As an atheist, Hawking has since searched (as shown by the second half of the quote) for an alternative to a universe with a finite beginning. I'll describe his efforts and those of other scientists. You decide how successful they've been in dealing with the monster. First, however, a quick review of the scientific method.

The Scientific Method

As mentioned earlier, Aristotle's science depended on reasoning alone. Following in Galileo's footsteps, modern science now tests theories with experimental data involving some or all of these methods: the observation of nature, classification of data, experimentation, logic, mathematical equations, and computer modeling. Through these methods, scientific advances come through chance, hard work, or sudden creative insights, but they all have this in common: a theory will not be accepted as scientific knowledge unless other researchers can verify it through repeated experiments.

The big bang theory involved all of these scientific methods. Furthermore, the data can be and have been verified by independent observers. In short, this is science at its best—solid and leaving no room to argue the data, only the conclusion.

Let's take a look at theories that try to deny a beginning point for our universe and the theological implications.

Other Theories

How about parallel universes?

If there are—as Carl Sagan said—"billions and billions" of other universes,[8] then from a mathematical and scientific point of view, remote as the possibility is, it can be a random accident that our universe, out of the infinite number of universes, just happened to hit on the right combination of fundamental forces that produced life. And, of course, our beginning is not really a beginning. Just part of a cycle that involves other universes.

But this supposition clearly steps outside the scientific method. A theory will not be accepted as scientific fact unless it can be verified through repeated experiments. This parallel-universe supposition, then, is convenient science-fiction speculation. Other universes have never been observed in practice. And it's beyond our reality to observe them in principle, as, by definition, they are outside our universe.

This theory also ignores the question of the causation of all the other parallel universes.

At one time, famous scientist John Wheeler was the most prestigious proponent of this theory. But he eventually stopped supporting it, saying, "There's too much metaphysical baggage carried along with it. . . . It makes science into some kind of mysticism."[9]

Um, yes.

All right, if believing in parallel universes takes as much if not more faith than looking for a supernatural Creator, how about turning to "baby" universes as an alternative?

That's led to another proposal: when a black hole is formed, new, baby universes can form with four space-time dimensions that exist at right angles to the existing universe. Documented in practice? Observable in principle? Causation issue addressed? None of the above. The idea fails the scientific method.

Let's move on.

How's this related series of premises by another scientist, John Gribbin, in his 1993 book, *In the Beginning*?

1. The earth is a single living organism.
2. Each galaxy is also, literally, a living entity.
3. Our universe is also alive.
4. Our universe was once a baby universe in another universe.

5. Our living universe is seeding other baby universes through black holes.
6. The purpose of the universe is to create black holes.

None of these assertions rests on any proven fact. Neither are they observable in practice or in principle. Nor does the proposal address the causation issue.

Enough said?

The solution of Stephen Hawking, perhaps our most respected living physicist, is to find a way to make the beginning not really a beginning. Hawking used the 1981 Vatican conference to introduce to the world his now-famous "no boundary" theory of the universe.

In the Hartle-Hawking no-boundary universe (Hawking refined his original theory with fellow scientist Jim Hartle), our universe exists within a larger superspace made of real and mathematically imaginary time. Here time is not linear but more like a sphere. Finding the beginning point in this sphere of real and imaginary time would be impossible, just as it would be impossible to define, geographically, where our planet begins.

Cosmology raises so many difficult questions regarding the creation of the universe that it might explain why atheists often turn to the theory of evolution to bolster their arguments. But even that is perilous ground for them . . .

In other words, this universe has a finite size but no boundaries to mark space and time.

Size but no boundaries?

In his book *A Brief History of Time*, Hawking does point out what should already be obvious: "This idea that time and space should be finite without boundary is just a proposal: it cannot be deduced from another principle. Like any other scientific theory, it may be initially put forward for aesthetic or metaphysical reasons."[10]

Look up *metaphysical* in your dictionary, and then make your own conclusions about Hawking's inability to deal with the overwhelming evidence that the universe began *creatio ex nihilo*.

This is Latin, of course. Creation out of nothing. That pesky Genesis account resurfaces again, to haunt atheist scientists.

Cosmology raises so many difficult questions regarding the creation of the universe that it might explain why atheists often turn to the theory of evolution to bolster their arguments.

But even that is perilous ground for them . . .

FOURTEEN

The Monster's Friend

In my view, DNA sequence alone, even if accompanied by a vast trove of data on biological function, will never explain certain special human attributes, such as the knowledge of the Moral Law and the universal search for God. Freeing God from the burden of special acts of creation [for each species] does not remove Him as the source of the things that make humanity special, and of the universe itself. It merely shows us something of how he operates.

—Dr. Francis Collins,
head of the Human Genome Project

If the origin of the human body comes through living matter which existed previously, the spiritual soul is created directly by God.

—Pope John Paul II

In July 2007, in the dark of early morning, two masked men with baseball bats smashed the windows of a vehicle on the street of an upscale Washington, DC neighborhood, punctured all the tires with a knife, and scratched a message on the side.

It was an act of vandalism that met with the apparent approval of many of the residents.[1] Theirs was a liberal, upscale neighborhood with Volvos and Toyota Prius hybrids. The damaged vehicle was a Hummer. The message was simple: "FOR THE ENVIRON."

Although the owner had saved for months to buy his treasured vehicle, as reported by the *Washington Post,* many people in the neighborhood drove past the crime scene and glared at the Hummer's owner in satisfaction. One neighbor, whose Prius gets 48 miles to the gallon compared to the Hummer's 14 miles per gallon, pointed out that "the neighborhood in general is very concerned with the environment . . . it's ridiculous to be driving a Hummer." Another neighbor suggested the owner needed to get a more "discreet and economical" vehicle.[2]

However, not all neighbors were as unsympathetic. One considered it a hate crime, and declared that the masked avengers have "everything at their disposal in this city to make a statement in a legal way."[3]

It was a polarizing incident, representing two major issues. The first is concern for the environment. The second is the freedoms and protections granted to American citizens by its self-chosen form of government.

Which emotional reaction hits you first? Resentment at Hummer owners and a small smile of satisfaction that one got what he deserved? Or anger that self-righteous environmentalists put their cause above of the law?

You might find this story to be a great starting point for an interesting discussion the next time you are with a group of friends. If you do use it, wait until the discussion is nearly over to reveal what seems to defy common sense and intuition:

The Hummer is almost twice as environmentally friendly as a Toyota Prius hybrid.

Evolution: the Smashed Hummer?

If the big bang theory is one monster in the closet, its best friend is the theory of evolution. But is this new monster a friend or foe to understanding that the universe was created by God?

Any polarizing debate about whether it was morally right to smash a Hummer's windshield is a mere whisper compared to the rhetoric and emotion vented during debates on evolution. If you piled up all the books for or against evolution that have been printed and sold since the topic was first introduced, the stack just might reach the moon, or at least to the space station.*

Opponents for and against the theory literally demonize one another. Passion and zeal, as best demonstrated by the Scopes trial, seem to matter more than knowledge.

> While this chapter is about evolution, it is not an argument for or against the validity of the science of the theory. Instead, it's about a way to approach what the science presents.

I might not be the first to suggest that these coffeehouse debates are much like the parable about blind men touching an elephant to learn what it is, each only handling one part, such as the trunk or the tail or the hide; the more knowledge you can bring to a subject, the closer to the truth your conclusion will be. I would also suggest that the less emotion you bring to the table, the better the chances of discerning the truth for yourself.

While this chapter is about evolution, it is not an argument for or against the validity of the science of the theory. Instead, it's about a way to approach what the science presents. It's about a tactic for opening dialogue with your children and, as honestly as

---

* I just made this up. It could be true though. And the metaphor certainly speaks to the truth of the statement.

possible, beginning to deal with the difficult intellectual questions that science might pose to believers or those seeking belief. It's about helping them respond to one of science's major theories in light of faith.

In the shadows of ignorance, the theory of evolution certainly appears to be a monster. Yet in the light of knowledge, you may see it is a different creature.

Before you unequivocally decide—for you or for your children—how to respond to the theory of evolution in light of a universe created by God, let's backtrack to the smashed-up Hummer.

A Matter of Perception

If your only reference point to environmental friendliness is fuel economy, then in the coffeehouse debate, the Prius is plainly the winner against the Hummer. Yet when you consider all the factors that go into a vehicle from "Dust to Dust"—from the first stage of manufacturing to the final disposal of a vehicle—a different truth begins to appear.

According to a *Globe and Mail* article that publicized the "world's most comprehensive analysis of the life cycle energy requirements of more than 100 makes and models of cars and trucks,"[4] the Hummer is 40 percent greener than the Prius. The report was completed by Oregon-based CNW Marketing Research Inc., and identified four thousand data points for each vehicle. Energy consumed was not simply evaluated by fuel economy. The data points covered the entire life cycles of vehicles—

> *"In the shadows of ignorance, the theory of evolution certainly appears to be a monster. Yet in the light of knowledge, you may see it as a different creature."*

from energy consumed in research and development to the energy consumed in junkyard disposal. The electrical energy needed to produce each pound of parts was also converted into greenhouse emissions.

As an example, for the Prius, according to the report, Toyota buys a thousand tons of nickel a year from a mine in Ontario, Canada, where it is shipped to Wales for refining, then to China for more processing, and finally to Toyota's battery plant in Tokyo. That's ten thousand miles of shipping via petrol-burning engines of locomotives and ships. Should that entire carbon footprint be ignored by self-righteous Prius owners?

In comparison, the Hummer shares its design, development, and manufacturing costs with other GM products, including the platform and power train, so that the energy-per-unit costs are much lower.

Final conclusion by CNW Marketing Research Inc? The lifetime energy requirement of a Hummer was $1.90 per mile versus the Prius at $2.86.

So there you go. Over the lifetime of a vehicle, the Hummer is far better for the environment than a Prius. Right?

Maybe not.

Know What It Says

In *The God Delusion*, evolutionary biologist Richard Dawkins writes, "Christians seldom realize that much of the moral consideration for others which is apparently promoted by both the Old and New Testaments was originally intended to apply only to a narrowly defined in-group. 'Love thy neighbour' didn't mean what we now think it means. It meant only 'Love another Jew.'"[5]

I confess my first reaction to this assertion was emotional, angry, indignant. Some of my response was due to the fact that the rest of his book seems so spiteful, and I was fed up with it.

My next reaction was to analyze Dawkins's statement for validity. Was there a footnote showing how scholars arrived at this viewpoint through historical context or translation from Aramaic or ancient Hebrew? No. Neither could I find reference to it anywhere on Google. (This doesn't mean that such a scholarly reference doesn't exist, but if it's there, it's obscure. All the more reason that Dawkins should, out of respect to readers, footnote this to prove it's not merely his contention.)

Then I applied what I knew from my own Bible reading. It wasn't difficult to find passages that directly contradicted Dawkins's outrageous claim. From the Old Testament: "And if a stranger dwells in your land, you shall not mistreat him. The stranger . . . shall be to you as one born among you, and you shall love him as yourself; for you were strangers in the land of Egypt" (Lev. 19:33–34 NKJV).

That directive hardly sounds like an in-group attitude. If this alone is not enough to refute Dawkins, Jesus Himself makes it very clear in Matthew 5:43–47: "You have heard that it was said, 'You shall love your neighbor and hate your enemy.' But I say to you, love your enemies, bless those who curse you, do good to those who hate you and pray for those who spitefully use you and persecute you. . . . And if you greet your brethren only, what do you do more than others? Do not even the tax collectors do so?" (NKJV).

There's more. Even those unfamiliar with the Bible know that the story of the Good Samaritan directly shows that "neighbors" means those in need, regardless of ethnic boundaries. In other words, Dawkins is right in quoting Jesus as saying "love thy neighbor," but totally wrong in asserting what it means.

The consequence of Dawkins's clearly inaccurate inter-pretations of this part of the Bible is that I have no respect for *any* biblical arguments that Dawkins tries to make. If he gets something this simple so obviously wrong, he certainly has no credibility with me when he begins statements like this: "Jesus, if he existed (or whoever wrote his script for him if he didn't) . . ."[6] Why should I accept Dawkins when he says that Jesus had "somewhat dodgy family values"?[7]

Before we can comment on whether the theory of evolution is right, we must be right about exactly what it says. Otherwise we lose our credibility in critiquing an established scientific belief.

If we agree on how bad it makes Dawkins appear to be so blatantly wrong about what Jesus said, it's equally important and fair to apply of the same to an evaluation of the theory of evo-lution. Before we can comment on whether the theory of evolution is right, we must be right about exactly what it says. Otherwise we lose our credibility in critiquing an established scientific belief.

A Matter of Semantics

After the *Globe and Mail* article broke to a national readership, I was fascinated as I followed the swelling Internet argument about Hummer versus Prius.

Quick to strike back was the Green Party of Canada, which pronounced, "The whole article is garbage."[8] One reason cited was the fact that the "Dust to Dust" study came from a marketing firm, not a science journal. As a skeptical reader, I recognized this as logical fallacy, often used in court to degrade statements by witnesses with criminal records. If it's true, it's true, regardless of the source. Conversely, if it's false, it's false, regardless of the source. Ergo, let's examine the declaration, not the source.

Another argument against the report seemed more worthy, and without fallacy: "It arrives at the artificially high cost for the Prius by assigning it an arbitrary lifespan of 100k miles, and a Hummer 300k miles. There are Prius being used as cabs that have 200k on them now."[9] This information tilted me toward concluding that arguments in favor of a Hummer were a smoke-and-mirrors trick.

But to be safe, I went to the Web site of the original report. It verified that 100,000 miles had been used as benchmark for the Prius, and 300,000 for the Hummer.

Unfair comparison, I thought. The Green Party is right. But I kept reading . . . and tilted in the opposite direction when I found this:

> The Prius was amortized over 100,000-plus miles for a number of reasons. The 100,000 mile life expectancy for Prius is time as well as distance sensitive. The historical data shows early Prius models were driven an average of only 6,700 miles per year (rounded). At that rate, the vehicle would require 15 years to reach 100,000 miles. It was our determination that it is highly unlikely the '05 or '06 Prius models would still be in active service let alone serviceable 15 years from today.[10]

In other words, as the report stated, the Prius is capable of 200,000 miles in theory and sometimes practice, but real life research showed that the vast majority of owners would never put more than 100,000 miles on the vehicle.

So, was it a fair comparison? Is the Hummer better for the environment than the Prius?

My suspicion—not tested by real life research—is that you could put twenty people in a room and give them all of the pros and cons, and half would agree on the Hummer, while, of course, the other half would find a way to disagree. But at least the argument would be based on facts, not mistaken assumptions and false parameters. No one in the room would be blindly grabbing tusks or trunks or tails and wondering what the beast was.

Likewise, to show respect for the search for truth and God, any discussion about evolution should begin with enough foundational knowledge to ensure an argument devoid of mistaken assumptions and false parameters.

> *I've heard believers snort with derision at the possibility that humans evolved from monkeys. Yet that's not what the theory asserts. Instead, it states that humans and monkeys share a common ancestor and, at some point, branched away from each other.*

In many of my informal conversations about Darwin's theory, I've heard believers snort with derision at the possibility that humans evolved from monkeys. Yet that's not what the theory asserts. Instead, it states that humans and monkeys share a common ancestor and, at some point, branched away from each other. Again, I'm not arguing here whether the theory is right. I'm saying it's important to be right about what the theory says. Christians who make pronouncements based on inaccuracies lose credibility, as do those who glibly state that the theory of evolution is just that: a theory, with the implication that theories are mere guesswork, unproven.

Hang on. Back to the *American Heritage Dictionary*. Here's how *theory* is defined in the English language:

1. A set of statements or principles devised to explain a group of facts or phenomena, especially one that has been repeatedly tested or is widely accepted and can be used to make predictions about natural phenomena.

2. The branch of a science or art consisting of its explanatory statements, accepted principles, and methods of analysis, as opposed to practice: *a fine musician who had never studied theory.*

3. A set of theorems that constitute a systematic view of a branch of mathematics.

4. Abstract reasoning; speculation: *a decision based on experience rather than theory.*

5. A belief or principle that guides action or assists comprehension or judgment: *staked out the house on the theory that criminals usually return to the scene of the crime.*

6. An assumption based on limited information or knowledge; a conjecture.[11]

In common conversation, we're accustomed to the last three definitions—"I have a theory that Joe doesn't count all his strokes in golf." For scientists, however, it's the first usage—as an example, "the *theory* of gravity," which everyone accepts as true—that precisely predicts most aspects of gravity and is generally accepted in the science world. As Dr. Collins writes, "Critics are fond of pointing out that evolution is 'only a theory,' a statement that puzzles working scientists who are used to a different meaning of the word."[12]

Because of my reaction to Dawkins's gross error about what Jesus said, I can relate to any scientist who expresses frustration at nonscientific believers guilty of incorrect assumptions about the theory of evolution. I would suggest, however, to any scientist that those incorrect assumptions are not malicious or deliberate. The same cannot be said for prominent scientists who are equally guilty of misrepresenting the theory of evolution. And, because of their eminence, they do far more damage to the search for truth than any amount of misguided believers.

With that in mind, it's time to introduce an agnostic scientist to make that point for me.

Agnostic Extraordinaire

Michael Ruse, author of *The Evolution-Creation Struggle*, is a philosopher of science at Florida State University. I think it's important to establish his agnostic worldview because it strengthens his criticism. No one can accuse him of being a layman believer, tilting at windmills in an attempt to defend the Bible or faith.

Ruse strongly supports the theory of evolution. But he just as strongly criticizes scientists who push Darwinian evolution beyond science into a social theory. Ruse states what many scientists are unwilling to acknowledge: "This is not just a fight about dinosaurs or gaps in the fossil record. This is a fight about different worldviews."[13] Ruse labels this worldview "evolutionism," saying it goes beyond the scientifically accepted platform of evolutionary science and loads social values onto it that don't exist in science. This, in effect, turns evolutionism into a religion in which "its proponents have been trying deliberately to do better than Christianity."[14]

Is there a better example of such a proponent than Richard Dawkins? As an evolutionary biologist and science writer, he first reached public prominence with a 1976 book titled *The Selfish Gene.* In 1982 came *The Extended Phenotype,* and in 1986, *The Blind Watchmaker: Why the Evidence of Evolution Reveals a Universe Without Design.* While these books make scientific arguments in favor of evolution, Dawkins's bias toward evolutionism became clearest in his 2006 best seller, *The God Delusion.*

Because of scientists like Dawkins, the result is that *evolution* and *evolutionism* tend to be treated as the same thing, both in the media and in arguments with creationists who have a legitimate worldview but are underequipped when it comes to arguing in the arena of science.

It's an insidious deception.

> Evolutionism . . . truly is an evil monster, all the more dangerous because it hides beneath the cloak of the science of evolution, which, like all science, is worldview neutral.

Evolutionism, I would argue, truly is an evil monster, all the more dangerous because it hides beneath the cloak of the science of evolution, which, like all science, is worldview neutral. It is a difficult monster to fight, especially given human tendencies toward *binary opposition.*

Opposites Don't *Always* Attract

Binary opposition refers to a pair of terms that are defined or differentiated by their opposition to each other.

Inside. Outside.

Presence. Absence.

Light. Dark.

Up. Down.

These terms don't come with a lot of emotional baggage, but they do show our instinctive method of searching for meaning via binary opposition—understanding something by what it is not. Binary opposition is not without emotional consequences, however, because we humans also tend toward allegiances defined by binary opposites. It's an us-versus-them strategy that, it can be argued, was important for survival in early human history. Look for the emotional baggage in these binary opposites:

> *Atheists [use] the science of evolution as a sword to fight for the worldview of evolutionism. To defend the opposing worldview, theists, often Christians, react by taking up their own sword against the science of evolution. Most often this sword goes by the name of* intelligent design. *For a theist, this is poor battle strategy, nearly always doomed to failure.*

Woman. Man.

Boss. Worker.

Republican. Democrat.

Gay. Straight.

Jew. Arab.

Israel. Palestine.

What does this have to do with evolutionary theory? Everything. When the worldview of "evolutionism" poses as the science of "evolution," the binary opposites clearly emerge.

Atheist. Theist.

En Garde!

Atheists are extremely skilled at using the science of evolution as a sword to fight for the worldview of evolutionism. To defend the opposing worldview, theists, often Christians, react by taking up their own sword against the true enemy—the worldview aspect of evolutionism—but mistakenly diverted to fight the worldview neutral science of evolution. Most often this sword goes by the name of *intelligent design*. For a theist, this is poor battle strategy, nearly always doomed to failure.

First, the battleground should be set where it belongs—worldview against worldview. Here, theists retain sure footing and have at their disposal many weapons other than science, arguments put forth by the greatest minds in history. At the same time, proponents of evolutionism have to acknowledge that they've been trying to hide behind evolution. It's a battleground where the theist's enemy is visible and not well armed.

But when theists insist on fighting science instead of worldview, the sword taken up by creationist Christians has proven to be inadequate against the sword of the science of evolution. Again, my point is not to argue for or against the science of evolution; I'm merely looking at the results of the sword clashes in public forums, not in gatherings of believers who hate the word *evolution*.

Dover, Pennsylvania, is probably the best recent example, where in 2005 a lawsuit was brought against a public school district for requiring the presentation of intelligent design as an alternative to evolution to explain the origin of life.

The public school district lost. This was the holding of the United States District Court for the Middle District of Pennsylvania:

Teaching intelligent design in public school biology classes violates the Establishment Clause of the First Amendment to the Constitution of the United States (and Article I, Section 3 of the Pennsylvania State Constitution) because intelligent design is not science and "cannot uncouple itself from its creationist, and thus religious, antecedents."[15]

Keep in mind that it was not an activist judge who ruled against the teaching of intelligent design in a public school. Judge E. Jones III, a Republican and a churchgoer, was appointed by George W. Bush.[16]

In his 139-page decision, Judge Jones concluded "that the religious nature of ID [intelligent design] would be readily apparent to an objective observer, adult or child."[17] Even more significant to a theist determined to use intelligent design as a sword against the science of evolution, Judge Jones did not rule on whether intelligent design is true but on whether it is appropriate in the field of science. This is what his ruling established:

> After a searching review of the record and applicable caselaw, *we find that while ID arguments may be true, a proposition on which the Court takes no position*, ID is not science. We find that ID fails on three different levels, any one of which is sufficient to preclude a determination that ID is science. They are: (1) ID violates the centuries-old ground rules of science by invoking and permitting supernatural causation; (2) the argument of irreducible complexity, central to ID, employs the same flawed and illogical contrived dualism that doomed creation science in the 1980's; and (3) ID's negative attacks on evolution have been refuted by the scientific community.[18]

This was a pivotal court case. In public schools—the arena for the minds of the next generation—it appears that the science of evolution was the victor against theism.

THE MONSTER'S FRIEND   179

Wrong. *Evolution* did not triumph. *Evolutionism* did, because the battle was focused away from it.

The parents who first convinced the school board to add intelligent design as an alternative to the theory of evolution would have been far better served to attack the evolutionism espoused within the teaching of evolution, on the grounds that if the philosophy of ID is ruled out, it is equally unscientific to inject the philosophy of evolutionism into a public-school science course.

But inject evolutionism they have, and ever since, because of binary opposition, atheists have been able to convince theists that the theory of evolution proves God does not exist. It's commonly seen as an either-or. *Either* you support evolution and a godless universe *or* you support creationism and a universe with God.

> The theory of evolution simply does not address the existence or nonexistence of God.

But these atheists are mistaken about what the theory of evolution states, and theists should focus the battle there instead of fighting the science—the theory of evolution simply does not address the existence or nonexistence of God.

What Evolution Doesn't Say

Atheist Richard Dawkins argues that "evolution fully accounts for biological complexity and the origins of humankind, so there is no more need for God."[19] Yet if you strip away the eminence and respect that Dawkins commands as a scientist who holds the Charles Simonyi Chair for the Public Understanding of Science at Oxford University,[20] the logical fallacy behind this is laughable, and one you would easily be able to explain to your teenagers.

Dawkins's premise that evolution accounts for human origins does not lead in any way to the conclusion that God is *not* behind it. Or, as Dr. Francis Collins put it, "while [Dawkins's] argument rightly relieves God of the responsibility for multiple acts of special creation for each species on the planet, it certainly does not disprove the idea that God worked out His creative plan by means of evolution."[21]

Now, Dr. Collins, with his evangelical worldview, cannot scientifically assert that God *did* use the mechanism of evolution to form mankind. But by the same token, Dawkins, with his atheistic worldview, cannot scientifically say that God did *not*.

I hope you'll find it worthwhile to read some quotes by Stephen Jay Gould. Known as "America's unofficial evolutionist laureate," Gould was an evolutionary biologist and science historian who spent most of his teaching career at Harvard, until his death from cancer at age sixty-two.[22]

While Gould was a self-proclaimed agnostic, he had little patience for the atheistic proclamations of evolutionism. Note his irritation at scientists who try to impose a worldview on science:

> To say it for all my colleagues and for the umpteenth millionth time: Science simply cannot by its legitimate methods adjudicate the issue of God's possible superintendence of nature. We neither affirm nor deny it; we simply can't comment on it as scientists. If some of our crowd have made untoward statements claiming that Darwinism disproves God, then I will find Mrs. McInerney [his third-grade teacher] and have their knuckles rapped for it.[23]

For the most part, we've been led to believe that evolution gives a scientific position that justifies atheism. It's simply not true. Gould, historian of science, goes on to write:

Darwin himself was agnostic . . . but the great American botanist Asa Gray, who favored natural selection and wrote a book entitled *Darwiniana*, was a devout Christian. Move forward 50 years: Charles D. Walcott, discoverer of the Burgess Shale Fossils, was a convinced Darwinian and an equally firm Christian, who believed that God had ordained natural selection to construct the history of life according to His plans and purposes. Move on another 50 years to the two greatest evolutionists of our generation: G. G. Simpson was a humanist agnostic, Theodosius Dobzhansky, a believing Russian Orthodox.[24]

Gould's conclusion: "Either half my colleagues are enormously stupid, or else the science of Darwinism is fully compatible with conventional religious beliefs—and equally compatible with atheism."[25]

I cannot say this strongly enough. The science behind the theory of evolution does not state that there is no God. The science of evolution is not an enemy to your child's faith. The real enemy is evolutionism. If you understand that, you will be much better prepared to help your child understand that science and faith can be harmonized, because even if Gould is correct in saying that scientists should not comment on God, there are legions of scientists who have made worldview decisions based on the breathtaking beauty of what they've discovered in science.

> *The science of evolution is not an enemy to your child's faith. The real enemy is evolutionism.*

For many, the science behind the theory of evolution has led them to God.

You may have noticed that I've avoided arguing for or against intelligent design, for or against evolutionary theory. Although, after much research, I've come to my own conclusion, I'm not interested in arguing sides here. There is a stack of books to the moon if you want arguments for either position.

It may seem disingenuous, but as my daughters grow older, that's the approach I want to take with them. It is more important to me that they understand the profound difference between the science of evolution and the false claims of evolutionism. It is also important that they see that there are Christian scientists who refuse to place themselves in the trap of binary opposition, where one must support either evolution or a universe with God. I will not argue the details for or against a harmony between God and evolution. But I will argue that it must have some merit if intelligent scientists at the top of their fields, who are as sincere in their faith as any Christian, can see harmony there. It's only fair to let our questioning children consider what the scientists have to say once a clear difference has been established between evolution and evolutionism.

Regardless of whether we agree with evolution, we must familiarize ourselves with it as a potential *ally to faith*. Dr. Francis Collins points out in *The Language of God* that "mountains of material, in fact entire library shelves, are devoted to the topics of Darwinian evolution, creationism and Intelligent Design. Yet few scientists or believers are familiar with the term 'theistic evolution' . . . yet theistic evolution is the dominant position of serious biologists who are also serious believers."[26] I highly recommend this book for those wishing to explore the matter of theistic evolution. In it, Collins admits:

The need to find my own harmony of the worldviews ultimately came as the study of genomes—our own and that of many other organisms on the planet—began to take off, providing an incredibly rich and detailed view of how descent by modification from a common ancestor had occurred. Rather than finding this unsettling, I found this elegant evidence of the relatedness of all living things an occasion of awe, and came to see this as the master plan of the same Almighty who caused the universe to come into being and set its physical parameters just precisely right to allow the creation of stars, planets, heavy elements, and life itself.[27]

This monster can be a friend.

IN THE END, regardless of how I harmonize faith and science for myself, I do know this with certainty: it doesn't matter to me whether Olivia and Savannah come to the truths of the Bible by choosing the foundation of a creationist view of Genesis (which embraces six twenty-four-hour days), an intelligent-design view of Genesis, or a theistic-evolution view of Genesis. After my life's journey, when I walk through heaven's gate, I just want to know that at the end of my daughters' journeys, they, too, will be there.

FIFTEEN

My Daughters' Journeys

Now we see but a poor reflection as in a mirror; then we shall see face to face.
Now I know in part; then I shall know fully, even as I am fully known.

—1 CORINTHIANS 13:12 NIV

As our family was flying from Nashville to Chicago once, with first-grader Olivia at the window, our jet descended into the thick cloud cover that had lain below us for most of the trip. Olivia's view was suddenly obscured by ominous, opaque gray. She clutched my hand.

"It's okay," I said. "We're going to land pretty soon."

"But how can the pilots see?" she asked. "How do they know where the airport is?"

I've never been a brave flyer. So to get past my fears, I learned what I could by reading and through conversations with pilots. One of the things that reassured me most was discovering that from about fifteen miles out, the plane's computer locks in on a signal that enables it to take the aircraft down the correct path to the runway. In addition, air traffic controllers mark the path of each plane and ensure that there will be no midair collisions. The instrument panels are sophisticated enough to show the altitude at all times. There's a warning system to alert pilots if they are approaching a mountainside. And so on.

I tried to reduce all of this to a simpler answer for my young daughter. "They can see through the clouds with radar," I said.

"What's radar?" Her grip was still tight on my fingers. "How can they see with radar?"

"Radar is invisible radio waves that bounce off things," I said. "It gives them a picture of what's ahead."

Silence. No lessening of the grip. She was looking out the window again at the opaque gray. She could tell the jet was moving fast, because she remembered when it took off, and how the houses below became tiny as we whizzed overhead.

"What's invisible?" she said. I could tell she was trying to hide her fear.

"Something you can't see."

"But if you can't see it, how can the pilots see it?"

"The radio waves make noise when the waves bounce off things." As those words came out of my mouth, I knew how little sense it made.

"Huh?"

"The noise of the waves makes a picture on their computer screen."

"If it's a wave, how does it go through the cloud? How does it make noise? Why don't we hear it?"

She was afraid, and I wished I could do a better job. "It's how bats fly at night without hitting anything," I said. "The waves aren't really waves; they are like . . ."

Now I was really stumped. What exactly were ultrasonic waves? I could have taken out some paper and tried to draw them, but would that have helped?

Olivia's experience was too limited to make sense of any of the scientific explanations I might give her. She had no reference points; the only way for her to eventually understand would be to begin with the most basic reference points and, through years of education, build upon them, adding more and more until we could both speak a common scientific language that would let her grasp how radar worked.

In the end I gave up. On trying to explain, not on trying to address her fear.

"Olivia," I said, "even if you don't understand how radar works, let me tell you why pilots use it."

She nodded.

"It's very important for them to land the airplane safely," I said. "They don't want anyone hurt. Pilots do this every day, and they are very good at landing."

More silence. More gazing out the window at the clouds. There was a large bumping sound—the sound that always startles me as the landing gear is lowered.

She squeezed my hand. "What was that, Daddy?"

"The wheels are down," I said. "They are getting ready to land."

"Even though they can't see the ground?"

"Yes, my love. I promise, if you wait a little longer, you'll see the houses again. Will you trust me on this?"

Her grip on my hand lessened. "Yes," she said. She kept looking out the window. Soon enough we broke through the cloud cover, and she saw the streets and buildings of our destination.

"You were right, Daddy," she said. "Thank you."

Playing God

Curiosity and creativity are so intertwined that sometimes it's difficult to distinguish one from the other. Since we were made in the image of God, the ultimate Creator, I can only believe that these aspects of our nature reflect His glory. We are designed to ask *how* and *why*.

Yet the question *how* is too often posed without the innocent curiosity that Savannah showed when she asked me who made the moon. *How* is often asked with the same sense of hubris that began the chasm between God and man: if we discover how something is made or done, that gives us the power to do the same. Tell us how to do the magic trick, and we can become magicians ourselves.

> How *is often asked with the same sense of hubris that began the chasm between God and man: if we discover how something is made or done, that gives us the power to do the same.*

Right now, physicists are constructing particle accelerators that may allow them to create infinitesimal black holes for infinitesimal moments of time.[1] That will take them one step closer to understanding how God brought forth this universe into time and place.

But is it also one step closer to trying to become God?

The Missing Link

From the simplest organisms upward, there is a gradual progression from simple to complex that has led some people to believe that a random process of evolution is responsible for the vast array of species that humans have cataloged.

It's not only in the fossil record. We can see it today among species still in existence. One-celled viruses. Bacteria. Worms. Jellyfish. Sharks with backbones. Turtles. Birds. Monkeys. Humans. Genus by genus, the species in each become more physically complex, more intelligent, better able to adapt. Yet only the most complex and intelligent of these species are able to do more than adapt to the environment. Few manipulate the environment around them; few use tools, even in the most rudimentary manner.

What strikes me in this overview of species is how the pattern of gradual progression breaks so exponentially when it reaches the most complex species of all—*Homo sapiens.*

I have no argument with the animal behaviorist who makes a case for the advanced intelligence or social behavior or communication skills of dolphins or monkeys. I cannot accept, however, that this brings the animals anywhere near human levels.

Monkeys can pick sticks off the ground to jab into ant piles or knock down low-hanging fruit. But the technological gap between this and assembling a rocket capable of bursting from Earth's gravity to go to the moon and back is almost beyond metaphorical description. A monkey may be able to smear paints in an apparent attempt to draw, but the next monkey won't learn anything from it. On the other hand, the latest computer projections state that within ten years we'll be able to store twenty-five million pages of information on a chip smaller than a postage stamp.

Put viruses at the beginning of the highway and jellyfish at mile marker one if you like. Monkeys are way up the road at the hundred-mile marker, with different species crowding every inch of pavement from the virus all the way to the monkey. Then nothing. Not until the shimmering ribbon of empty asphalt has stretched long past the horizon. Then, finally, humans. All alone. Created, as no other species was, in the image of God.

What I'd like my daughters to wonder is the *why* of this. If we live in a universe that has produced us by naturalistic evolution without God, on an earth produced in the same way, why aren't there any creatures filling in the gap? Why did the progression break? Why are we so totally alone on the highway, past the horizon, looking back at the gap that puts us so far ahead that we are now capable of destroying every creature behind us, along with the planet that sustains us?

I'd like them also to wonder—in considering this exponential species gap—whether humans have souls.

Why are we the only species capable of creating music and writing and painting and ballet? Why are we the only ones capable of the emotions that come with hearing music or reading novels or seeing paintings or watching ballet?

Why are we so aware of our mortality? And so afraid of it?

The Bible gives us those answers, beginning with Genesis.

A Matter of Reference

In reading the first chapters of Genesis, I always marvel at the simplicity and elegance of the language used for the Creation account. I marvel, too, that these qualities have survived the different translations over the millennia that have passed since the ancients were first inspired to give us this account.

I've tried to imagine the Creation story divinely inspired to satisfy third-millennium readers who are impatient to understand how God created the world. A Genesis that gives a thorough mechanical explanation for those who cannot believe in a supernatural Creator unless the construction of the universe is laid out for them like a cake recipe or a wristwatch blueprint. A Genesis that includes concepts such as gravity, the strong and weak nuclear forces, and electromagnetism.

But I can't see it written any other way than it was.

It comes down to reference points. Words are powerful but are still nothing more than symbols. Words are often more effective as metaphors than as literal descriptions, but even then words may fail, because metaphors demand a common base of understanding between the teller and the listener. I discovered this as I tried to describe to Olivia how radar works.

Should Genesis have been written any other way?

Even though we live in a culture that trusts and almost worships science, the language of science is still far too specialized to allow most twenty-first-century readers to understand how the universe began. It's inconceivable, then, that the first audiences of the Genesis account could have understood God's description of Creation without the use of their language, their metaphors, and their reference points. If people today have no interest or difficulty with the basic science of high school or first year university, how much more difficult would it have been for Moses to explain it to the Israelites? Science, as a discipline or pursuit, did not exist for them. The Genesis account suited them perfectly, and it does the same for us.

> *What matters more than* how *we were created is* Who *created us and* why.

The Heart of the Matter

What matters more than *how* we were created is *Who* created us and *why*.

For Olivia, on the airplane, as we descended into the cloud that made her so afraid, she needed to know less of how radar worked and more of why. What she needed most was to know whether she could trust radar and trust my promise that it would help the pilots land our plane safely.

I believe that once we understand and trust the Genesis account in line with the purpose for which it was written, we need no longer fear the opaque gray that blocks our view of what happens on the other side of life. The clouds will break. We'll see our final destination, knowing fully then what now we only know in part.

And we will land safely.

Appendix A

Recommended Resources

Because *Who Made the Moon?* is intended neither as pure apologetics nor pure science, I'd like to first recommend *The Language of God* by scientist Francis Collins as a complement to this volume. Dr. Collins's book is what I hope this one will become: something to pass along to friends who are searching for God. (I have already bought and given away numerous copies of it.) While I will never try to force my daughters to believe what I believe, I will require them to read it when they are old enough. *The Language of God* makes it very difficult for an open-minded reader to become or remain an atheist.

While all of the books below have valuable, interesting information, please don't read these—or any other resources— without also using your critical thinking skills. *Learn. Grow. Stretch.* But be wise. Some of these authors do not view the world

ith that you do, and how they present
ced by their perspectives.

ry

Books

Dr. Francis Collins, head of the Human

orical Memoir of Science, Faith and Love

y Alister McGrath and Joanna Collicutt

What on Earth Am I Here For? by Rick

Convergence of Scientific and Biblical
L. Schroeder
Reconciliation of Faith and Reason in a
y Patrick Glynn
e? by Charles Colson and Nancy Pearcy
son by Jonathan Hill
The Scopes Trial and America's Continuing
e and Religion by Edward J. Larson
Jesus the Messiah by Alfred Edersheim
by Hank Hanegraaff
niverse: The Cosmos Explained by David

me by Stephen Hawking

more resources and discussion at
ww.whomadethemoon.com

came

0000
han
eit,
rce

nds
ees
he
ly

he

Timeline of the Big Bang St

In the beginning—There was a moment when nothing
something. Christians believe this happened because of G

10^{-43} *(0.000000000000000000000000000000000*
01) seconds after the big bang—the entire universe was smal
a single atom, and the temperature was 10^{33} degrees Fah
where all of existence was pure energy, not matter. The on
in the universe at this point of birth was gravity.

10^{-35} *(0.000000000000000000000000000000001,*
after the big bang—The universe cooled to 2×10^{28}
Fahrenheit, and the strong nuclear force emerged from wit
shadows of gravity. Matter didn't exist in any form yet
energy existed.

10^{-11} *seconds (0.00000000001) after the big bang*

universe cooled to 20 quadrillion degrees Fahrenheit (20 x 10^{16} degrees). Electromagnetism and the weak nuclear force uncoupled from gravity and the strong nuclear force.

10^{-5} seconds (0.00001) after the big bang—The universe cooled enough for energy to begin to convert to matter. The first subatomic particles formed, particles that would eventually give rise to electrons and protons and neutrons, which would then form atoms.

Three minutes after the big bang—The universe cooled to a few billion degrees. Protons and neutrons were able to bond and form the first nuclei of the three smallest atoms: hydrogen, helium, and lithium.

Twelve minutes after the big bang—The energy that permitted nuclei to fuse could no longer be sustained. These were the only three elements in the early universe. The other eighty-nine natural elements would have to wait until billions of years later, when stars and supernovas would generate the heat to forge them.

Three hundred thousand years after the big bang—The universe cooled to about four thousand degrees. Electrons finally were able to settle into orbit around the nuclei, and the elements are formed. Gravity began to clump matter as part of an extremely long process of building stars until enough hydrogen was massed for the gravitational forces to ignite nuclear fusion and begin burning the stars. Then the galaxies of these stars formed.

A billion years after the big bang—The large-scale structure of the universe was set.

Then came supernovas, stars old enough and big enough to burn themselves into a spectacular collapse at high enough temperatures to form new elements, spewing forth all these elements that would make planets, including our own solar system. As this material clumped in our own solar system, Earth was formed in such a way that water and atmosphere would sustain life.

Discussion Points for Children

Although this book was written for adults and at a level that adults can discuss with teenagers, at some point the adults might want to discuss these concepts with younger children. Here are some sample chapter-by-chapter scripts that might help you explain some important points to kids.

CHAPTER 1—WHO MADE THE MOON?

Your questions about where the moon, the dinosaurs, and people came from are good, important questions. I'm proud of you for wanting to know and understand God's world better. These big questions are ones that people throughout history have been asking, and they've come up with a lot of very different answers. Some people discover more about how amazing God is, while other people decide that there is no God. In my own search for answers I've come to believe more and more strongly in God, and I'll be happy to help you explore your questions.

Chapter 2—Through Heaven's Gate

Throughout your whole life, you will hear or read a lot of things that will make you wonder about God. You might wonder whether He really loves you or whether you'll go to heaven. You might wonder whether everything in the Bible is true. It's okay to wonder. The important thing is that when you wonder about God or you wonder about the Bible, you must not give up. God does love you very much, and He wants to answer all your questions. It just might take awhile for you to understand everything He's trying to teach you. Nothing—absolutely nothing—is more important to me than someday being together with you and the rest of our family in heaven. If you're ever worried or wondering, please come to me. I won't try to make you believe everything exactly the way I believe, but I can help you make sense of whatever is confusing you. I love you. Always! No matter what!

Chapter 3—Intellectual Honesty

Only a really brave person asks the big questions and dares to seek honest answers. I'm proud of you for being so brave, and I'm so glad that you told me about your questions. It sometimes seems like science and the Bible can't both be right, but the truth is that God actually uses *both* science and the Bible to teach us special things about Himself and about the amazing world He's given us. God loves us very much, and He would never try to trick us. Instead, He wants us to know Him. He's bigger than all our big questions, and if you and I search for the answers together, then we'll be able to see more of the special things God wants to show us. As we search, we might find some answers that make us a little bit uncomfortable, but we'll be brave together until we get to the truth.

CHAPTER 4—PHYSICS AND THE MIRACLE OF LIFE

You are a miracle. No, really. You are! It's not just that you're such a good, smart, funny person. I know you're a miracle because the science that tells us about the universe also tells us that it's very, very, very unlikely that you or me or anyone else should ever have existed in the first place. A famous mathematician estimated that the scientific stuff at the beginning of time had less than a one in 10^{123} chance of ever producing life. This is a 1 followed by 123 zeros. It would take you billions of years to count to that high a number. Another prominent scientist said that the chance of conditions essential to life happening by accident is about the same as billions of blind people solving a Rubik's Cube all at the same second. Many people—including scientists and including me— believe something that rare can only be a miracle. This is one way that science shows us how powerful and smart God is. So, you see, you really are a miracle. Don't let anyone ever tell you otherwise.

CHAPTER 5—IN THE BEGINNING

Light travels very fast. But stars are so far away that the light from those stars has taken hundreds, thousands, and millions of years to reach our eyes here on Earth. With powerful telescopes, looking outward at the edges of the universe is like looking back in time.

Scientists have taken hundreds of years to interpret what the universe tells us, and they are finally concluding what Genesis has told us all along: the universe had a beginning point and a beginning place.

For a long time, many people who don't believe in God did not want to believe this about the universe, because it meant they would have to consider that the universe was a creation.

Chapter 6—Creatio Ex Nihilo

You can't create something out of nothing. And nothing that exists can continue existing forever. That should mean there should not be a universe. Science now shows that billions of years ago the universe apparently was created out of nothing, but science cannot explain how that happened. For many people, this means that we have to look outside of natural forces to explain how something came from nothing—in other words, how the universe was created by something or someone supernatural. Like God!

Chapter 7—The Foundations of the Earth

As science shows us, the beginning of the universe was an amazing event! Like a tiny, tiny balloon suddenly appearing out of nowhere, except exploding bigger and hotter than thousands of suns.

It is so breathtaking that scientific language doesn't really give us an idea of what this means. Instead, by using the beautiful language of the Bible, we can have the smallest of inklings of what it was like when God laid the foundations of the earth.

Chapter 8—In Galileo's Footsteps

People have struggled with whether to believe science or faith for a very long time. More than four hundred years ago the great scientist Galileo Galilei was put on trial for teaching that the earth goes around the sun. The leaders of the church had always believed that the sun went around the earth, and they were afraid to think about his new ideas. They were afraid that if people started to believe the church was wrong about this one thing, then the people would begin to question everything else. Well, even though Galileo spent the rest of his life under house arrest, he never stopped trusting in God. Galileo always believed that everything science discovered was just another way of getting to know God better, and his courage still inspires other people to seek answers through science too. Like Galileo, people today can use science to find out about God. Because God created this universe, all science comes from Him, and the more we learn, the more we're about to find Him there.

CHAPTER 9—THE FENCE AROUND THE CROSS

One of the ways that people often try to end arguments is by saying they'll agree to disagree. People say, "I believe what I believe, and you believe what you believe, and we'll still get along just fine even though we believe different things." This can be a very helpful way to think when people bring up how science seems to disagree with the Bible. Always remember that many, many wise people have studied this issue, and they still come to a lot of different answers. What the Bible says about the beginning of the world definitely confuses people when they compare it to what science says, but here's something that I want you to keep in mind: the Bible also clearly tells us to live in peace with one another. It clearly tells us to bring other people to know Jesus. This doesn't mean you should just be a doormat for other people's opinions about our origins, but it does mean that whatever you come to believe about the Creation, you're even more responsible for teaching people about Jesus and for helping people come to the Cross. Keep your cool. Don't get angry when other people disagree with you. Respect them, even when they don't respect you. Yes, I want you to be smart about Creation and what it means to

ays were actually ages in which millions of years passed. And
people think the whole creation account is a parable that
symbolism to tell a very complicated scientific story to people
didn't understand science. One reason people have so many
rent ideas about this important passage is because some of the
s can have slightly different meanings. For instance, the
ent Hebrew word for "day" is *yôm*, which could mean either
twenty-four-hour period or it could mean a much longer time.
ause we can't go back in time to view the beginning of the world,
can't know exactly. What's important for you to realize is that
ether you decide to believe in six regular-length days of creation
n six general eras of creation, "in the beginning, God created the
vens and the earth." All interpretations of the Bible agree on
s, and more and more science points to this conclusion.

HAPTER 12—MISUNDERSTANDINGS OF SCIENCE

Any discussion—whether about science, religion, people,
usic, or whatever—can become complicated or even angry if
eople don't agree on a few things in the beginning. We need to
se the same definitions of words. For instance, if I ask, "Did you
lean your room?" in order for you to answer correctly, you need
o understand whether "clean" means it's safe to walk in your
oom without tripping over stuff or whether "clean" means every-
hing is put away, the floor is vacuumed, and your bed is made
a good discussion, it's also important to understand how
everybody knows about the topic. If you say, "I like t'
but you've only heard a few seconds of one song
don't have enough knowledge to make a wis
you've heard all their songs and read their
views with the band members while the
then you're making a more informed state.

everyone's role in the universe, but, even mo[...]
wise about the Cross and what it means t[...]
eternity. Be prepared to understand and disc[...]
about the beginning of the world. But please[...]
even better prepared to understand how what y[...]
whether someone goes to heaven.

CHAPTER 10—MAN WITHOUT GOD

How we view where we came from affect[...]
everything else about ourselves, such as whethe[...]
valued or intended for some special purpose in lif[...]
began to question whether God created us, they[...]
doubt that He cared about us. They began to thin[...]
just a cosmic accident, people with no real value or [...]
grand scheme of things. This depressing outlook h[...]
the way people have been thinking about things fo[...]
hundred years. But recent discoveries in science hav[...]
the universe does, in fact, have a beginning. In th[...]
something came from nothing, and no natural law[...]
how that beginning point happened. It has to have[...]
outside of nature. This beginning point supports the B[...]
that God made the universe. This reassures us that He[...]
He does love us, and He does have a special plan for us[...]

CHAPTER 11—MISUNDERSTANDINGS OF THE BIBLE

Wise people throughout the world have been stud[...]
Bible for thousands of years, and although on many poi[...]
eople agree, there are still some things that cause pe[...]
gree. The Creation is one of those passages where peop[...]
different opinions. Some people think the story is l[...]
six regular twenty-four hour days, while other people[...]

everyone's role in the universe, but, even more, I want you to be wise about the Cross and what it means to everyone's role in eternity. Be prepared to understand and discuss many opinions about the beginning of the world. But please make sure you're even better prepared to understand how what you say could affect whether someone goes to heaven.

CHAPTER 10—MAN WITHOUT GOD

How we view where we came from affects how we view everything else about ourselves, such as whether we're loved or valued or intended for some special purpose in life. When people began to question whether God created us, they also started to doubt that He cared about us. They began to think that we're all just a cosmic accident, people with no real value or purpose in the grand scheme of things. This depressing outlook has dominated the way people have been thinking about things for the past few hundred years. But recent discoveries in science have shown that the universe does, in fact, have a beginning. In the beginning, something came from nothing, and no natural law can explain how that beginning point happened. It has to have come from outside of nature. This beginning point supports the Bible's claim that God made the universe. This reassures us that He does exist, He does love us, and He does have a special plan for us.

CHAPTER 11—MISUNDERSTANDINGS OF THE BIBLE

Wise people throughout the world have been studying the Bible for thousands of years, and although on many points most people agree, there are still some things that cause people to disagree. The Creation is one of those passages where people have very different opinions. Some people think the story is literally about six regular twenty-four hour days, while other people think the days were actually ages in which millions of years passed. And other people think the whole creation account is a parable that uses symbolism to tell a very complicated scientific story to people who didn't understand science. One reason people have so many different ideas about this important passage is because some of the words can have slightly different meanings. For instance, the ancient Hebrew word for "day" is *yôm*, which could mean either one twenty-four-hour period or it could mean a much longer time. Because we can't go back in time to view the beginning of the world, we can't know exactly. What's important for you to realize is that whether you decide to believe in six regular-length days of creation or in six general eras of creation, "in the beginning, God created the heavens and the earth." All interpretations of the Bible agree on this, and more and more science points to this conclusion.

CHAPTER 12—MISUNDERSTANDINGS OF SCIENCE

Any discussion—whether about science, religion, people, music, or whatever—can become complicated or even angry if people don't agree on a few things in the beginning. We need to use the same definitions of words. For instance, if I ask, "Did you clean your room?" in order for you to answer correctly, you need to understand whether "clean" means it's safe to walk in your room without tripping over stuff or whether "clean" means every- thing is put away, the floor is vacuumed, and your bed is made. In a good discussion, it's also important to understand how much everybody knows about the topic. If you say, "I like this band," but you've only heard a few seconds of one song, you probably don't have enough knowledge to make a wise decision. But if you've heard all their songs and read their lyrics and seen inter- views with the band members while they were doing charity work, then you're making a more informed statement. It's also important that you don't assume that everyone sees things the same way. If you ask someone, "What's the best pet?" Their answer may depend on whether they have a big yard where a dog can run, a small apartment that's cozy for a cat, or allergies that mean they can only have fish. It helps to understand a lot of things before beginning even a regular conversation, and it's even more important to understand the common ground before talking about topics as complicated as science or the Bible. Many, many disagreements about evolution and creation happen simply because people don't establish the common ground before they start talking. That's one of the reasons I want you to keep talking to me about all this stuff—I really want to understand everything you're saying so we can explore your questions and find good answers together.

Chapter 13—The Monster in the Closet

Many Christians are afraid to study what science says about the big bang, because they're afraid that would be disrespectful to God and would go against the Bible's story of Creation. But the truth is that the big bang actually points to God instead of away from Him. It's a basic scientific law that something can't come from nothing, and something—or Someone—outside of science's laws had to start the big bang. There's no need for Christians to be afraid of the big bang theory; in fact, many people are afraid of this theory because it forces them to think about God even if they don't want to believe in Him. Yes, there are scientists who believe in theories other than the big bang. They talk about parallel universes, baby universes, living universes, unbounded universes, and other ideas that make for fun science fiction stories but have no proof in scientific fact. Instead, the overwhelming evidence in nature is that somehow, in the beginning, everything came from nothing a process that can only be adequately explained by God's supernatural power.

CHAPTER 14—THE MONSTER'S FRIEND

Remember when we talked about how important it is for people to understand each other's definitions before trying to have a good conversation? That's very, very important when we talk about the theory of evolution. To scientists, a "theory" is something that has been tested, evaluated, studied. It's something that they think should be commonly accepted as fact, such as the theory of gravity. To nonscientists, a "theory" is largely guesswork. It's a possibility, not a fact, such as the theory that a person who was caught running away from one robbery also should be a suspect in another robbery.

We need to understand the evidence for the theory of evolution—even if we don't agree with it—because this evidence is taught as science fact. The data is usually reliable, even if we disagree with the conclusions. Where things go wrong, though, is when people confuse *evolution* with *evolutionism. Evolution,* at its core, is a scientifically analyzed process of how things change, while *evolutionism* is a philosophical approach to putting science in the place of God. The theory of evolution itself is not the enemy of people who believe in God; the worldview of evolutionism is. The theory of evolution doesn't say one way or another whether there is a God; it's the worldview of evolutionism that uses some science and some philosophy to say there is no God. Even one of the most famous atheists of modern times said, "the science of Darwinism is fully compatible with conventional religious beliefs—and equally compatible with atheism." The science of evolution isn't a danger to our faith; the conclusions people draw from it is.

This is part of every modern person's journey; you have to learn about the science, learn about the Bible, and try to decide for yourself how evolution and Creation might or might not work together as one beautiful story of God's amazing design for this world. This is a tough topic, and some of your friends probably will choose different answers, but I'll help you however I can. Also, you're probably learning new science that wasn't known when I was in school, so I know you can teach me some things. You're not alone in this quest to understand. Let's learn together.

CHAPTER 15—MY DAUGHTERS' JOURNEYS

As smart as monkeys and dolphins are, they're nowhere close to humans. We're so far advanced beyond them that there's no question—we are a special species, set apart from all other animals. Although many people may look at all the scientific evidence and decide that humans and monkeys once shared a common ancestor, we're not the same now. God gave us the Creation story in Genesis to assure us that He has given us everything we need—light, water, food, relationships, His Spirit, and more—and even if we believe that it is just a simple parable for a complex series of scientific processes, it's still enough. It still reminds us that we are people who are loved by God, designed for His purpose, and blessed with the gift of freedom to make our own choices about what to believe. How we were created is less important than Who created us. We came from God, and now He lovingly draws us back to Himself. And being home with Him someday is the only thing that really, really matters.

Notes

CHAPTER 1

1. Richard Dawkins, *The God Delusion* (New York: Houghton Mifflin Company, 2006), 5.
2. "Atheist Becomes Theist: Exclusive Interview with Former Atheist Antony Flew," *Biola News & Communications*, http://www.biola.edu/antonyflew/page2.cfm. For more on Antony Flew, see Chapter 3.

CHAPTER 2

1. http://www.carm.org/creeds/apostles.htm.
2. Ask Bill Nye, http://encarta.msn.com/encnet/features/columns/?article=BNAllergies.
3. John 14:2 NKJV.
4. Richard Dawkins, *The God Delusion* (New York: Bantam, 2006); Chris Hedges, *American Fascists: The Christian Right and the War on America* (New York: Simon & Schuster, 2008); James Rudin, *The Baptizing of America: The Religious Right's Plans for the Rest of Us* (New York: Thunder's Mouth Press, 2006); Sam Harris, *The End of Faith: Religion, Terror and the Future of Reason* (New York: W.W. Norton & Co., 2004); David Mills with Dorion Sagan, *Atheist Universe: The Thinking Person's Answer to Christian Fundamentalism* (Berkeley, CA: Ulysses Press, 2006).
5. Daniel Lapin, "A Rabbi's Warning to U.S. Christians," WorldNetDaily, January 13, 2007, http://www.wnd.com/news/article.asp?ARTICLE_ID=53748.

6. Andrew Keen, *The Cult of the Amateur: How Today's Internet Is Killing Our Culture and Assaulting Our Economy* (New York: Currency, 2007)

7. Ibid.

8. C. S. Lewis, "Is Theology Poetry?" in *The Weight of Glory and Other Addresses* (New York: Harper Collins, 1980), 140.

9. Alister McGrath and Joanna Collicutt McGrath, *The Dawkins Delusion?* (Downers Grove, IL: InterVarsity Press, 2007), 97.

10. Francis S. Collins, *The Language of God: A Scientist Presents Evidence for Belief* (New York, Free Press, 2006), 145–46.

11. Rick Warren, *The Purpose Driven Life: What on Earth Am I Here For?* (Grand Rapids: Zondervan, 2003), 11.

12. Ibid., 17.

13. Augustine, *The Literal Meaning of Genesis 20:40.* (Westminster, Maryland: Newman Press, 1982).

14. Ibid.

15. C. S. Lewis, *The Problem of Pain* (New York: Simon & Schuster, 1996), 71.

16. Jon Meacham, "Pilgrim's Progress," *Newsweek*, August 14, 2006, 41.

CHAPTER 3

1. Collins, *The Language of God*, 33.

2. "Atheist Becomes Theist," http://www.biola.edu/antonyflew/page2. cfm.

3. Ibid., http://www.biola.edu/antonyflew/index.cfm.

4. Ibid.

5. You can find a general overview in Gerald L. Schroeder's book, *The Science of God: The Convergence of Scientific and Biblical Wisdom* (New York: Broadway Books, 1997)

6. "Atheist Becomes Theist," http://www.biola.edu/antonyflew/page6. cfm.

7. Collins, *The Language of God*, 178.

8. C. S. Lewis, *Surprised by Joy* (New York: Harcourt Brace, 1955).

CHAPTER 4

1. *The American Heritage Dictionary of the English Language*, 4th ed., s.v. "miracle."

2. J. Horgan, "Heart of the Matter," *Scientific American*, December 1993.

3. Schroeder, *The Science of God*, 186.
4. Fred Hoyle, *The Intelligent Universe* (New York: Holt, Rinehart and Winston, 1983), 11.
5. Brandon Keim, "Physicist Neil Turok: Big Bang Wasn't the Beginning," *Wired*, February 19, 2008, http://www.wired.com/science/discoveries/news/2008/02/qa_turok
6. Brandon Carter, "Large Number Coincidences and the Anthropic Principle in Cosmology," in M. S. Longair, ed., *Confrontation of Cosmological Theories with Observational Data* (Dordrecht: D. Reidel, 1974), 291–98.
7. Bertrand Russell, *Religion and Science* (Oxford: Oxford University Press, 1960).
8. "Four Fundamental Interactions," 9 August 2000, www.lbl.gov/abc/wallchart/chapters/04/0.html.
9. Fred Hoyle, "The Universe: Past and Present Reflections," *Engineering and Science*, November 1981, 8–12.
10. Stephen Hawking, *A Brief History of Time* (New York: Bantam Books, 1988), 120–21.
11. Paul C. Davies, *The Accidental Universe* (Cambridge, UK: Cambridge University Press, 1982), 90.
12. Fred Hoyle, *The Origin of the Universe and the Origin of Religion* (Wakefield, RI: Moyer Bell, 1993), 19, emphasis added.
13. Physics 110, "Age of the Universe," www.cs.csubak.edu/Physics/phys110/UniverseScale.html.
14. Charles Colson and Nancy Pearcy, *How Now Shall We Live?* (Wheaton, IL: Tyndale House, 1999), 66.
15. Patrick Glynn, *God: The Evidence: The Reconciliation of Faith and Reason in a Postsecular World* (Roseville, CA: Prima Publishing, 1999), 54.

CHAPTER 5
1. David Filkin, *Stephen Hawking's Universe: The Cosmos Explained* (New York: HarperCollins, 1997), 96.
2. Ibid., 85–86.
3. Ibid.
4. Eric W. Weisstein, "Einstein, Albert (1879–1955)," World of Scientific Biography, http://scienceworld.wolfram.com/biography/Einstein.html.
5. Filkin, *Stephen Hawking's Universe Explained*, 86.

Chapter 8

1. Brian Becker, "Maria Celeste's Birth Certificate and Horoscope," The Galileo Project, http://galileo.rice.edu/fam/birth_horoscope.html.

2. Dava Sobel, "Maria Celeste (Virginia) Galilei (1600–1634)," The Galileo Project, http://galileo.rice.edu/fam/maria.html.

3. Bertrand Russell, *History of Western Philosophy* (London: George Allen & Unwin, 1946), 182.

4. Galileo Galilei, "Letter to the Grand Duchess Christina of Tuscany, 1615," Modern History Sourcebook, http://www.fordham.edu/halsall/mod/galileo-tuscany.html.

5. Colson and Pearcy, *How Now Shall We Live?*, 69.

6. Bryan Mendez, "Lecture 5," Astronomy 10: Introduction to General Astronomy, Summer Session 2000, Session A, University of California, Berkely, http://cse.ssl.berkeley.edu/bmendez/ay10/2000/notes/lec5.html.

7. "Galileo Galilei," Cordis, http://cordis.europa.eu/scienceweek/inspiration02.htm.

Chapter 9

1. Jeanne Bendick, *Along Came Galileo* (Sandwich: Beautiful Feet Books, 1999), 62.

2. Jonathan Hill, *Faith in the Age of Reason* (Downers Grove: Intervarsity Press, 2004), 119.

3. "Westminster Theological Seminary and the Days of Creation: A Brief Statement," http://www.wts.edu/about/beliefs/statements/creation.html. Visit this Web site to read the conclusions of scholars who have wrestled with the "days of creation."

4. Hugh Ross, *A Matter of Days*, (Colorado Springs: NavPress, 2004).

5. Moses Maimonides (1135–1204) was a twelfth-century rabbi and was considered to be one of the foremost philosophers in Jewish history.

6. Edward J. Larson, *Summer for the Gods: The Scopes Trial and America's Continuing Debate over Science and Religion* (New York: Basic Books, 1997), 189.

7. Ibid., 190.

8. Ibid., 191.

9. Ibid., 242.

10. Ibid., 244.

11. Intelligent design was formulated in the 1990s, primarily in the United States, as an explicit refutation of the Darwinian theory of biological evolution. Building on a version of the argument from design for the existence of God, proponents of intelligent design observed that the functional parts and systems of living organisms are "irreducibly complex" in the sense that none of their component parts can be removed without causing the whole system to cease functioning. From this premise they inferred that no such system could have come about through the gradual alteration of functioning precursor systems by means of random mutation and natural selection as the standard evolutionary account maintains; therefore, living organisms must have been created all at once by an intelligent designer. Proponents of intelligent design generally avoided identifying the designer with the God of Christianity or other monotheistic religions, in part because they wished the doctrine to be taught as a legitimate scientific alternative to evolution in public schools in the United States, where the government is constitutionally prohibited from promoting religion. Critics of intelligent design argued that it rests on a fundamental misunderstanding of natural selection, that it ignores the existence of precursor systems in the evolutionary history of numerous organisms, and that it is ultimately untestable and therefore not scientific. *Encylopedia Britannica*, s.v. "intelligent design," [www.britannica.com/eb/article-9432671/intelligent-design]
12. Larson, *Summer for the Gods*, 190.

CHAPTER 10
1. Cover of *Time*, April 8, 1966.
2. Colson and Pearcy, *How Now Shall We Live?*, 52.
3. "Double Helix is a double cross to the reader," Amazon.com Customer Reviews, http://www.amazon.com/Double-Helix-Sigmund-Brouwer/dp/customer-reviews/0849912156.
4. Bertrand Russell, *Religion and Science* (Oxford: Oxford University Press, 1961; originally published 1935), 216.
5. Schroeder, *The Science of God*, 19.
6. Ibid., 3.

CHAPTER 11
1. Alfred Edersheim, *The Life and Times of Jesus the Messiah* (Peabody, MA: Hendrickson Publishers, 1993), 347–48.

2. Meacham, "Pilgrim's Progress," 41.

3. So, how do you read and understand the Bible with confidence to avoid misunderstandings? To decide when the author is literal and when the author is figurative?

   You take the time to learn more about how the Bible was written.

   I'll happily plug *The Apocalypse Code* by Hank Hanegraaff, with whom I've coauthored several books.

   Hank presents the acronym LIGHTS to use as an approach to any biblical passage. It's an acronym that, on one hand, shows the effort that should go into reading the Bible for all it is worth, and on the other, demonstrates how easy it is to learn the true intent of the divinely inspired authors. This is how Hank explains it:

   L: *Literal principle.* Simply put, this means that we are to interpret the Word of God just as we interpret other forms of communication—in its most obvious and natural sense. Thus, when Scripture uses a metaphor, we should interpret it accordingly.

   I: *Illumination principle.* "We have not received the spirit of the world but the Spirit who is from God, that we may understand what God has freely given us" (1 Corinthians 2:12 NIV). The Spirit of truth not only provides insights that permeate the mind, but also provides illumination that penetrates the heart. Clearly, however, the Holy Spirit does not supplant the scrupulous study of Scripture. Rather, He provides us with insights that can only be spiritually discerned. Put another way, the Holy Spirit illumines what is *in* the text; illumination does *not go beyond* the text.

   G: *Grammatical principle.* As with any literature, a thorough understanding of the Bible cannot be attained without a grasp of the basic rules that govern the relationships and usages of words.

   H: *Historical principle.* The Christian faith is historical and evidential. Thus, the biblical text is best understood when one is familiar with the customs, culture, and historical context of biblical times. Such background information is crucial in fully grasping what is going on in any given book of the Bible.

T: *Typology principle.* In terms of a proper end-times paradigm, this principle is of paramount importance. In Scripture *types* symbolize persons, places, or things that are axiomatic to redemptive history. For example, circumcision of the flesh is typological of circumcision of the heart. Thus says Paul, "A man is not a Jew if he is only one outwardly, nor is circumcision merely outward and physical. No, a man is a Jew if he is one inwardly; and circumcision is circumcision of the heart, by the Spirit, not by the written code" (Romans 2:28–29 NIV).

S: *Scriptural synergy.* Simply stated, this means that the whole of Scripture is greater than the sum of its individual passages. You cannot comprehend the Bible as a whole without comprehending its individual parts and you cannot comprehend its individual parts, without comprehending the Bible as a whole. As such, individual passages of Scripture are synergistic rather than deflective with respect to the whole of Scripture.

Scriptural synergy demands that individual Bible passages may never be interpreted in such a way as to conflict with the whole of Scripture. Nor may we assign arbitrary meanings to words or phrases which have their referent in biblical history. The biblical interpreter must keep in mind that all Scripture, though communicated through various human instruments, has one single Author. And that Author does not contradict Himself nor does He confuse His servants.

4. Collins, *The Language of God,* 175.
5. "Circular reasoning," English 1101/55 and 57, Kennesaw State University, Fall 2002, http://ksuweb.kennesaw.edu/~shagin/logfal-pbc-circular.htm.
6. Meacham, "Pilgrim's Progress," 41.
7. Ibid.
8. "Report on the Creation Study Committee," PCA Historical Center, http://www.pcahistory.org/creation/report.html.
9. Kenneth A. Mathews, *The New American Commentary; Genesis 1–111:26,* (Nashville: B&H Publishers), 149.
10. Shroeder, *The Science of God,* 60.
11. Ibid., 67.

CHAPTER 13

1. Sir Arthur Eddington, "The End of the World: From the Standpoint of Mathematical Physics," *Nature* 127 (1931), 450.
2. Filkin, *Stephen Hawking's Universe Explained*, 131.
3. Colson and Pearcy, *How Now Shall We Live?*, 59.
4. Hawking, *A Brief History of Time*, 46.
5. Glynn, *God: The Evidence*, 41.
6. Ibid., 40.
7. Hawking, *A Brief History of Time*, 140–41.
8. Carl Sagan, *Billions and Billions: Thoughts on Life and Death at the Brink of the Millennium,* (New York: Ballantine, 1998) 3–4.
9. Quoted in P. C. W. Davies and J. R. Brown, *The Ghost in the Atom* (Cambridge, UK: Cambridge University Press, 1993), 60.
10. Hawking, *A Brief History of Time*, 136.

CHAPTER 14

1. Allison Klein, "Hummer Owner Gets Angry Message: Vandals Batter D.C. Man's SUV, Slash Its Tires and Scratch in an Eco Note," *Washington Post*, July 28, 3007, B01, www.washingtonpost.com/wp-dyn/content/article/2007/07/17/AR2007071701808.html.
2. "Vandals Smash, Scratch 'Eco' Message Into Hummer," http://www.msnbc.msn.com/id/19836967/ (no longer available).
3. Klein, "Hummer Owner Gets Angry Message."
4. Neil Reynolds, "Which Cars Are the Greenest? You'd Be Surprised," *Globe and Mail*, July 27, 2007, http://www.theglobeandmail.com/servlet/story/RTGAM.20070727.wreynolds0727/BNStory/Business/columnists.
5. Dawkins, *The God Delusion*, 253.
6. Ibid., 250.
7. Ibid.
8. Adam King, "Hummer More Environmentally Friendly Than Hybrid Prius?" Green Party, July 28, 2007, http://www.greenparty.ca/en/node/2410.
9. Ibid.
10. CNW Reasearch, "Why 100,000 miles for Prius," CNW's Dust-to-Dust Automotive Energy Report, April 2007, http://cnwmr.com/nss-folder/automotiveenergy/.
11. *The American Heritage Dictionary of the English Language*, 4th ed. Houghton Mifflin Co., s.v., "theory," http://dictionary.reference.com/browse/theory.
12. Collins, *The Language of God*, 142.

13. Peter Dizikes, "Evolutionary War," *Boston Globe*, May 1, 2005, www.boston.com/news/globe/ideas/articles/2005/05/01/evolutionary_war?pg=full.

14. Ibid.

15. Delia Gallagher and Phil Hirschkom, "Judge Rules Against 'Intelligent Design' in Science Class," *CNN*, 23 December 2005. www.cnn.com/2005/LAW/12/20/intelligent.design/index.html.

16. Ibid.

17. *Kitzmiller v. Dover Area School District*, http://www.pamd.uscourts.gov/kitzmiller/kitzmiller_342.pdf, 24.

18. Ibid, emphasis added.

19. Collins, *The Language of God*, 163.

20. *Wikipedia*, s.v. "Richard Dawkins," http://en.wikipedia.org/wiki/Richard_Dawkins.

21. Collins, *The Language of God*, 163.

22. *Wikipedia*, s.v. "Stephen Jay Gould," http://en.wikipedia.org/wiki/Stephen_Jay_Gould.

23. Steven Jay Gould, "Impeaching a Self-Appointed Judge" (a review of Phillip Johnson's *Darwin on Trial*), *Scientific American* 267, no. 1 (July 1992): 118–21.

24. Ibid.

25. Ibid.

26. Collins, *The Language of God*, 199.

27. Ibid.

CHAPTER 15

1. Craig Freudenrich, PhD., "How Atom Smashers Work," http://science.howstuffworks.com/atom-smasher.htm.

About the Author

Best-selling author Sigmund Brouwer has written 18 novels and several series of children's books. A champion of literacy, he teaches writing workshops at schools from the Arctic Circle to inner-city Los Angeles. Sigmund is married to recording artist Cindy Morgan, and they and their two daughters divide time between homes in Red Deer, Alberta, Canada and Nashville, Tennessee.

Who Made the Moon?
Study/Discussion Guide

This discussion guide is designed to help you grasp the key thoughts found in *Who Made the Moon?* For each chapter in the book you will find a corresponding discussion section with several features: a *Main Idea* entry summarizes the primary point of each chapter; *Key Questions* revisits the central questions posed in each chapter; *Key Concepts* asks you to ponder the core ideas of each chapter; *Key Wisdom* offers a short Bible study on issues covered in each chapter. The discussion guide is suitable for either group study or individual reflection.

CHAPTER 1: WHO MADE THE MOON?
Main Idea: We must be prepared to answer questions raised by modern science that some individuals may use to try to dismiss a vital faith in God.

Key Questions:
1. What's so important about the question, "Who made the moon?"
2. How would you answer the question, "Why are we able to share love?"
3. How would you answer the question, "Where does this love come from?"

Key Concepts:
1. Name some important implications of the statement, "God made the moon."
2. Do you agree that the Bible gives answers to all of the major questions of human existence? Why or why not?

Key Wisdom:

1. Read Genesis 1–2.
   A. Does this passage try to "prove" the existence of God? What is significant about this?
   B. What picture of God do you get from reading this passage?
2. Read Psalm 19:1–6.
   A. What do the heavens teach us about God?
   B. What do the heavens *not* teach us about God?
3. Read Romans 1:20.
   A. What does creation tell us about God?
   B. What is important about this knowledge?

CHAPTER 2: THROUGH HEAVEN'S GATE

Main Idea: The primary responsibility for preparing children to make a vital faith commitment to Christ lies at home.

Key Questions:

1. How would you deal with losing one of *your* children for eternity?
2. What is "out there" that encourages your children to doubt a Christian worldview?
3. Especially where it concerns the faith of your children, do you think it's more important to find points of agreement between science and Genesis, rather than highlighting points of possible disagreement? Explain.
4. What do you think of Saint Augustine's statement regarding the Creation account that, "What kinds of days these were, it is extremely difficult, or perhaps impossible for us to conceive"?
5. How do you respond to Dr. Billy Graham's admission that he is open to considering that the word *day* in Genesis may be used in a figurative sense?

Key Concepts:

1. Do you agree that, "A primary responsibility for helping children judge truth must begin at home"? Why or why not?

2. In what ways is "everything colored by the answer you give to the question, 'Does God exist?'"

3. Why is it "futile and impossible to attempt to extinguish the false beacons in this world"?

4. How do you respond to Rick Warren's statement, "If you want to know why you were placed on this planet, you must begin with God. You were born *by* his purpose and *for* his purpose"?

Key Wisdom:

1. Read 2 Timothy 1:3–5.
   A. What does the apostle Paul imply about his own religious upbringing?
   B. What does Paul imply about Timothy's religious upbringing?
   C. What implications does this passage have for the way you rear your own children?

2. Read Ephesians 6:4.
   A. To whom is this verse directed? Why is that significant?
   B. What instruction is given here? How are you carrying out this instruction?

3. Read Deuteronomy 6:4–9.
   A. To whom is this passage directed? What is its purpose?
   B. In what venues should such instruction take place? What does this fact imply about the nature of this instruction? How are you carrying out this instruction?

Chapter 3: Intellectual Honesty

Main Idea: Our children will follow Christ gladly only when they make that choice of their own volition and in their own time; it cannot be forced.

Key Questions:

1. If God Himself refuses to force His children to choose Him, then why should we futilely and wrongly attempt to force *our* children to choose Him?

2. If doubt is wrong, then why was God so patient with Job?

3. How have you responded so far to your own children's struggles with faith and doubt? Does your handling of these struggles make it more or less likely that they will turn to you when they face other important issues in life in the future?

Key Concepts:

1. How do you respond to the statement, "Jesus showed that He is more interested in helping the followers on the road to the cross with Him, than wasting energy on converting someone who has made a decision against the cross"?

2. Do you agree with the statement, "If I don't let my children challenge my views with their doubts, they'll never really accept what I believe"? Why or why not?

3. How can you help your children come to the point that when they read the Bible, it is not you speaking to them, but God?

4. What good can come out of discussing doubts?

5. How do your children know that you love them and will accept them no matter what?

Key Wisdom:

1. Read Deuteronomy 30:19–20.
    A. What is the choice presented here?
    B. Why must it be a real choice?

2. Read Joshua 24:14–15.
    A. What does Joshua urge the people to do here?
    B. What choice does Joshua give the people?
    C. How can this pattern inform your own practice at home?

3. Read Proverbs 1:29–33
    A. What choice is highlighted here?
    B. What is the result of choosing poorly?
    C. What is the result of choosing wisely?
    D. How can the results of choices be used to influence future choices?

CHAPTER 4: PHYSICS AND THE MIRACLE OF LIFE

Main Idea: The odds against life arising on earth by chance are, statistically speaking, colossal. The existence of life points to a Designer.

Key Questions:

1. Why is there something rather than nothing?
2. Is it so ridiculous to think that this world is moved by an invisible hand? That something—or Someone—created it?
3. How probable is it that you could win the lottery ten weeks in a row? Twenty weeks in a row? Every week for a year? How do you react to the idea that you have a better chance of enjoying such a winning streak than that the universe would generate human life simply by chance?

Key Concepts:

1. Respond to the following statements: "I should not be here. Neither should you. This planet should not exist either. Nor the sun. Nor any matter in the universe. That we are here is a miracle in the truest sense."
2. What do you think of the idea that, "Perhaps everything has been arranged around one central task: producing humankind"?
3. What difference does it make that, "If any of the four fundamental forces is altered in the slightest, everything in the universe literally falls apart?"
4. Do you agree or disagree with the following statement: "The mathematical probability of the staggering number of physics coincidences it takes for a life-sustaining universe to exist cannot be reasonably accounted for by randomness"? Explain.

Key Wisdom:

1. Read Psalm 104:24–27.
   A. How does the Creation show God's wisdom?
   B. How is God connected to His Creation?
2. Read Psalm 148.

A. How does the psalmist think we should respond to God's creation?

B. How does the psalmist reveal his own study of God's creation?

3. Read Colossians 1:15–18.

A. In what way is Creation of theological importance?

B. How does Christ continue to relate to His creation?

CHAPTER 5: IN THE BEGINNING

Main Idea: Modern science theorizes that the universe began with "the big bang."

Key Questions:

1. Why did so many scientists resist the idea of a moment of creation?

2. Why did the "steady state" concept of the universe stand in direct opposition to any account that told us God was responsible for Creation?

3. If the universe did burst forth from nothing, would you expect to see some evidence of this event? Why or why not?

4. Why is looking further and further into the outer regions of the universe like looking back into ancient time?

5. Why does the "redshifting" of distant stars indicate that they are traveling away from us at high speed? Why is this important?

Key Concepts:

1. What is the significance of the following statement: "Genesis, like cosmology, tells us that the universe did indeed burst forth from nothing"?

2. Explain the significance of the following statement: "Hubble and his team discovered that not only was the universe expanding in all directions, but it was an accelerated expansion!"

3. Describe your reaction to the following statement: "By knowing how far the galaxies were from Earth and one another at different points in time, it became possible to calculate when all the galaxies had been together, some 15 billion years earlier."

4. Explain the scientific importance of the following: "In every
   direction they looked in outer space, it was 3° Kelvin—only three
   degrees above absolute zero. And so the telephone company
   researchers had accidentally stumbled across what the Princeton
   academics had been trying to find: Hoyle's fossil of the big bang."

Key Wisdom:
1. Read Psalm 90:2.
   A. What does this verse tell us about the relationship between God
      and His Creation?
   B. Why is this significant?
2. Read Proverbs 8:22–31.
   A. How does the writer picture "wisdom" in this passage?
   B. How does "wisdom" respond to God's work of creation?
3. Read John 17:5, 24.
   A. What personal claims is Jesus making in these two verses?
   B. How do these verses color your understanding of Creation?

CHAPTER 6: CREATIO EX NIHILO
Main Idea: The existence of "black holes" helps us to understand what
happened in the big bang.

Key Questions:
1. What is a "black hole"? How is it created? How does it affect
   matter and energy around it?
2. Why is the existence of black holes so important to the theory of
   the big bang?
3. Is it crazy to believe that at one time all the matter of the universe
   was packed into a point of nothingness? Explain.

Key Concepts:
1. What is significant about the following statement: "The visible
   matter of this universe comprises only 10 percent of all matter
   that exists"?

2. What is significant about the following statement: "Nothing in science can speak to the causation of the singularity. It is outside the realm of the natural laws that govern this universe"?

Key Wisdom:
1. Read Isaiah 55:8–9.
   A. Why is it important to keep the message of this passage in mind?
   B. What does this passage suggest about our legitimate attempts to understand Creation?
2. Read Job 38:31–33; 42:1–3.
   A. What is the point behind God asking Job these questions?
   B. How does Job respond? What does this suggest in regard to our own intellectual grasp of the universe?

CHAPTER 7: THE FOUNDATIONS OF THE EARTH
Main Idea: A theoretical timeline of what happened immediately after the big bang helps us to appreciate God's wonder of Creation.

Key Questions:
1. Does the big bang theory bolster your belief that God exists? If so, why? If not, why not?
3. Do current cosmological findings and theories affect your understanding of Genesis 1–2? Explain.
4. Why can science tell us nothing about "the awesome moment when space and time were brought into being"?

Key Concepts:
1. Describe your response to the following statement: "Accepting an older earth, for me, does not dispute the Genesis account."
2. What thoughts and feelings did you become aware of as you read about what scientists believe happened in the first moments after the big bang?
3. How do you respond to the following statement: "Like Job, I can

only tremble and wonder in awestruck amazement at how God laid the foundations of the earth"?

Key Wisdom:
1. Read Job 31:35–37; 38:4–7.
   A. What request does Job make? How does God honor that request?
   B. Does the encounter unfold as Job expected? Explain.
2. Read Proverbs 3:19–20.
   A. What attribute of God is emphasized here? Why is this important?
   B. What should contemplating the Creation remind us about God?
3. Read Hebrews 1:10–12.
   A. What claim is made in verse 10?
   B. What contrast is made in verse 11?
   C. What prophesy and promise is made in verse 12?

CHAPTER 8: IN GALILEO'S FOOTSTEPS
Main Idea: The story of the sixteenth-century astronomer Galileo helps us to see how good science can strengthen faith, rather than weaken it.

Key Questions:
1. Would you be apt to consider Galileo a "hero of the faith"? Why or why not?
2. Would you agree that, "The Bible is not a science manual but a divinely inspired history meant to show the reason for God's relationship with the human race"? Explain.
3. Do you believe that, "God gave us the brains and curiosity to learn what He didn't feel was necessary to teach in the Bible"? Explain.

Key Concepts:
1. Why do you think that, "Galileo's honest pursuit of science never led him to doubt his Creator"?
2. What "dogmas" do you think science insists upon today?

3. How do you respond to the following statement: "The Bible is a book about how one goes to heaven, not about how heaven goes"?

4. Do you agree that, "A little science estranges a man from God, but a lot of science brings him back"? Explain.

5. Discuss the following statement: "Galileo's verified scientific data had no dispute with the Bible or the existence of God. The dispute arose because of the nonbiblical claims of church leaders."

Key Wisdom:

1. Read 1 Corinthians 4:6 (NIV).
   A. How do you interpret the warning, "Do not go beyond what is written"?
   B. How would heeding this warning have lessened conflict in Corinth?

2. Read John 21:20–23.
   A. How did Jesus respond to Peter's question?
   B. How did others misinterpret Jesus' response?
   C. What lessons does this incident have to teach us?

CHAPTER 9: THE FENCE AROUND THE CROSS

Main Idea: Insisting on a young earth, contrary to the volumes of data amassed by modern science, makes it much harder to have fruitful discussions of faith with seekers and others.

Key Questions:

1. Do you believe the world was created in six literal days? Explain.

2. Is the ability to reason part of what it means to be made in God's image? If so, then is rejecting this ability any different from choosing to throw away the gift of vision by wearing a blindfold?

3. Should we tell our friends and coworkers who are beginning to seek God to ignore modern science and take everything on faith?

4. If our friends—or our children—reject what the Bible teaches because they cannot get past an apparent conflict between science and Genesis, then how will we see them in heaven?

Key Concepts:

1. How do you respond to the following statement: "Any creationist who advocates a young-earth view will have considerable difficulty persuading most listeners outside of his or her church circles that there is a Creator"?

2. Do you agree with the following statement: "Conflicts between science and the Bible result from a lack of scientific knowledge or a defective understanding of the Bible"? Explain.

3. What do you think Sigmund means by the following statement: "Creationism did not lose at the Scopes trial. Only the person who represented it did"?

4. How can you "Be prepared, not overconfident," in discussions of faith and science?

Key Wisdom:

1. Read Galatians 2:11–14.

   A. What conflict erupted between Paul and Peter?

   B. How did this conflict act as a "fence around the cross"?

2. Read 2 Corinthians 5:20—6:3.

   A. What kind of "ambassador" did Paul consider himself to be?

   B. What kinds of "stumbling blocks" could keep Paul from his mission?

3. Read Romans 14:4–5, 13.

   A. How are believers in Christ to treat one another when they disagree on some disputable issue?

   B. What are believers in Christ *not* to do when disagreements arise?

CHAPTER 10: MAN WITHOUT GOD

Main Idea: If God does not exist, then humankind has no more significance than dirt.

Key Questions:

1. Could something as complicated as a dragonfly be the product of a random universe, brought into being by strictly naturalistic means?

2. What is your role and relationship with God? What is your purpose?

3. How can you help others to understand the God of Scripture and His promise of the Cross?

Key Concepts:

1. In your own words, describe "naturalism, the dominant worldview in Western culture today."

2. Do you think it's true that, "Without God, humans have no more importance than dirt"? Explain.

3. Do you think it is true that, "Today's science is not unfriendly to a created universe"? Explain.

4. How do you respond to the following statement: "If you avoid a subjective bending of the Bible to match science, or of science to match the Bible, science becomes a strong ally of faith"?

Key Wisdom:

1. Read Psalm 14:1.

   A. What picture does this text paint of humankind without God?

2. Read Romans 3:9–18.

   A. What picture does this text paint of humankind without God?

   B. How does this picture correspond with the one painted in 2 Timothy 3:1–5?

CHAPTER 11: MISUNDERSTANDINGS OF THE BIBLE

Main Idea: A failure to understand biblical passages in their historical and literary context can lead to unnecessary disputes with science.

Key Questions:

1. Do you believe it is possible for "sincere Christians to discuss" the issue of the age of the earth "openly and without rancor"? Explain.

2. Where does the Bible use figurative language? Give several examples. Where does it use literal language? Give several examples.

3. Do you believe it "would have served God's purpose thirty-four

228 WHO MADE THE MOON?

hundred years ago to lecture to his people about radioactive decay, geologic strata, and DNA"? Explain.

Key Concepts:
1. In order to "avoid misinterpreting the Bible," why is it necessary to "first understand that it is a divinely inspired book, made of a rich tapestry containing many assorted writing genres"?
2. How do you respond to the following statement: "The last few decades in science have brought us much, much closer to God"?
3. What do you think Sigmund means by the following statement: "Don't use the Bible to argue science. But use science to argue the Bible, and you won't be defeated"?

Key Wisdom:
1. Read Nehemiah 8:1–8.
   A. Why did the people gather at this occasion?
   B. What is so important about verse 8?
2. Read 2 Timothy 2:15.
   A. What charge did Paul give to Timothy?
   B. What is important for us about this charge?

CHAPTER 12: MISUNDERSTANDINGS OF SCIENCE
Main Idea: Effective critical thinking depends on avoiding errors in four crucial areas: definitions; parameters; assumptions; and perspective.

Key Questions:
1. What do you think science can tell us about the nature of God?
2. Do you believe we are "merely cosmic debris belched forth from the stars, the products of a random universe"? Explain.
3. What do you understand by the terms, "definitions," "parameters," "assumptions," and "perspective"?
4. Do you believe we were "created with souls engineered for union with God in this life and beyond"? Explain.

Key Concepts:
1. Do you agree that, "The Bible is not a science manual"? Explain.
2. How do you respond to the following statement: "The interpretation of data generates volumes of argument, because data can suggest a variety of conclusions"?
3. How is it possible that "Inarguable data can lead to arguable conclusions"?
4. Do you agree that, "Truth is indivisible"? Explain.

Key Wisdom:
1. Read James 1:19.
   A. What are believers in Christ to be "quick" to do?
   B. What are they to be "slow" to do?
   C. How does this counsel relate to legitimate differences in biblical interpretation?
2. Read Titus 3:9.
   A. What are believers in Christ to "avoid"?
   B. Why are they to avoid them?

CHAPTER 13: THE MONSTER IN THE CLOSET

Main Idea: Christians should consider the big bang theory their friend, not their enemy.

Key Questions:
1. Why was the big bang theory so repugnant to some scientists?
2. What is the major difficulty some Christian readers of Genesis have with the big bang theory?
3. Without God, how can one explain the moment when the universe first burst into time and space from nothing?

Key Concepts:
1. Why do you think that, "Some scientists may find it difficult, as do many outside of science, to have faith in something that cannot be quantified"?

2. How do you respond to the following statement: "If God created humankind, then we are lesser beings"?

Key Wisdom:
1. Read Hebrews 11:1–3, 6.
   A. How does the Bible describe "faith"?
   B. What is the first example of "faith" mentioned in this passage?
   C. Why is faith necessary for pleasing God?
2. Read Psalm 8.
   A. How does the psalmist picture humankind in this passage?
   B. Who is the central figure in this passage? How is He described? How is this significant for us?

Chapter 14: The Monster's Friend
Main Idea: We must learn to recognize the huge difference between the science of evolution and the false worldview of evolutionism.

Key Questions:
1. How would you define the science of evolution?
2. How would you define the worldview of evolutionism?
3. Do you think that evolution is a friend or foe to understanding that God created the universe? Explain.

Key Concepts:
1. What do you think Sigmund means when he writes, "Dawkins is right in quoting Jesus as saying, 'love thy neighbor,' but totally wrong in asserting what it means"?
2. How do you respond to the following statement: "Before we can comment on whether the theory of evolution is right, we must be right about what exactly it says"?
3. Do you think it is true that, "Christians who make pronouncements based on inaccuracies lose credibility"? Explain.
4. In what way is "all science worldview neutral"?
5. Comment on the following statement by the late Stephen Jay

Gould: "Science simply cannot by its legitimate methods adjudicate the issue of God's possible superintendence of nature. We neither affirm nor deny it; we simply can't comment on it as scientists."

Key Wisdom:
1. Read Psalm 147:4–5, 8-11.
   A. What picture of God do you get in verses 4–5 and 8–10?
   B. Could you say that the Lord "delights" in you (v. 11)? Explain.
2. Read Deuteronomy 29:29.
   A. What things belong to God?
   B. What things belong to us? What purpose do they serve?

CHAPTER 15: MY DAUGHTERS' JOURNEYS
Main Idea: The enormous gap between human beings and all other creatures suggests that *Who* created us, and *why*, is more important than *how* He created us.

Key Questions:
1. If we live in a universe that has produced us by naturalistic evolution without God, then why aren't there any creatures filling in the gap?
2. Why are we the only species capable of creating music and writing and painting and ballet? Why are we the only ones capable of the emotions that come with hearing music or reading novels or seeing paintings or watching ballet?
3. Why are we so aware of our mortality? And so afraid of it?
4. Should Genesis have been written in any other way?

Key Concepts:
1. What does it mean for you that, "we are designed to ask *how* and *why*"?
2. How do you respond to the following statement: "What matters more than *how* we were created is *Who* created us and *why*"?

3. Do you think it is true that, "Once we understand and trust the Genesis account in line with the purpose for which it was written, we need no longer fear the opaque gray that blocks our view of what happens on the other side of life? Explain.

Key Wisdom:
1. Read Psalm 32:6–10.
   A. What promises does God make in this passage?
   B. What negative comparison do you see in verse 9?
   C. What is the great privilege of being human, given to no others?
2. Read 1 Corinthians 2:6–10.
   A. What is the difference between knowledge and wisdom?
   B. For whom has God reserved indescribable things?